DOMESTICITIES

At Home with The New York Times Magazine

DOMESTICITIES

At Home with The New York Times Magazine

Pilar Viladas

Bulfinch Press

New York • Boston

Copyright © 2005 by The New York Times Company

All rights reserved. No part of this book may be reproduced in any form or by any electronic or mechanical means, including information storage and retrieval systems, without permission in writing from the publisher, except by a reviewer who may quote brief passages in a review.

Bulfinch Press

Time Warner Book Group
1271 Avenue of the Americas, New York, NY 10020
Visit our Web site at www.bulfinchpress.com

First Edition: November 2005

The articles on which much of this book is based originally appeared in *The New York Times Magazine* and, to the extent such articles are reprinted here, they are reprinted with permission. Inquiries concerning permission to reprint any such articles or portions thereof or any photographs should be directed to The New York Times Company, News Services Division, The Times Agency, Ninth Floor, 229 West 43rd Street, New York, New York 10036 or rights@nytimes.com.

Library of Congress Cataloging-in-Publication Data

Viladas, Pilar.
   Domesticities : at home with the New York Times magazine / Pilar Viladas.—1st ed.
       p. cm.
   ISBN 0-8212-5710-2
  1. Interior decoration—United States. I. New York Times. II. Title.
NK2004.V54 2005
747'.0973—dc22

                                                                2004027941

Design by Hotfoot Studio

PRINTED IN SINGAPORE

To the architects and designers who created these
residences, the clients who commissioned them,
and the photographers who captured them on
film — you all make the world a little safer for beauty.

Contents

MODERN LIVING...101

PERSONALITY PROFILES...159

INTRODUCTION

We are living at a time when Americans' interest in the home — in building it, renovating it, and decorating it — is at a high point. So it is no surprise that many people are fascinated by design. But it is welcome news to people like me, for whom the subject is a passion, if not an obsession.

When I was growing up, I loved to look at other people's houses — in person, in books, in movies, and on television. In fact, I've retained memories of these rooms long after I've forgotten who was in them or even where I saw them. I can tell you where I was the first time I sat on a down cushion — a sinking sensation both luxurious and alarming. I can describe Doris Day's perfect decorator's apartment and Rock Hudson's bachelor pad in the film *Pillow Talk;* Rosalind Russell's often-redecorated duplex in *Auntie Mame;* or Kay Kendall and Rex Harrison's stylish drawing room in *The Reluctant Debutante.* I could take you on a room-by-room tour of a friend's elegant, beautifully decorated brick Georgian-style house — even though the house was sold years ago. Little did I know then that one day I would be looking at other people's houses — and writing about them — for a living.

In the more than eight years that I've been at *The New York Times Magazine*, we have featured all kinds of houses and apartments of almost every stylistic stripe. We have visited houses big and small, modest and grand, retro and cutting edge. What matters is not the size or style of someone's home but whether it has a story to tell. As an editor and writer, I find that the hardest question a reader can ask me is "What are the trends today?" At the beginning of the twenty-first century, a better question might be to ask what isn't a trend, because we live in a time when eclecticism rules. I believe that a more important consideration is how well a particular designer or architect has absorbed design's history, as well as its present, and synthesized it into something with a personality of its own.

The last time a selection of home stories from the *Times Magazine* was published in book form was in Norma Skurka's 1976 volume, *The New York Times Book of Interior Design and Decoration*. The book, which is now eagerly collected by design aficionados, offered a comprehensive and astute look at — and a valuable photographic record of — the work of the best designers of the time.

The houses and apartments in this book represent what is happening in the worlds of architecture and decorating today, but just as important, they are personal, sometimes idiosyncratic portraits of the people who designed them or live in them. Sometimes those people are one and the same; about half the dwellings shown on these pages are designers' own homes — largely because they tend to be vivid, unrestrained self-portraits in addition to being skillfully designed. All the residences in this book have something to teach us, in addition to providing the sheer pleasure of looking at them.

THE NEW CLASSICS

Americans have long played fast and loose with tradition. They like to honor the past while living wholeheartedly in the present and looking toward the future. That sense of pragmatism got us neighborhoods stocked with mini-Tudor and mini-Georgian manors, small-scale French châteaus, suburban Spanish colonial haciendas, and tract-house Early American saltboxes — most of which were built in this country from the 1920s through the 1960s. (A more recent, unfortunate mutation of this outlook, fed by soaring real estate prices, has produced the McMansion, that graceless pastiche of historical styles that is invariably built far too large for its small but costly suburban lot.)

Today, more than ever, tradition isn't what it used to be. After all, the history of architecture and design now includes the entire twentieth century, and a very eventful hundred years it was, encompassing (among others) the Vienna Secession and art nouveau, the Arts and Crafts movement, International Style modernism, the French 1940s, midcentury modernism, the swinging sixties, the funky seventies, the opulent eighties, and the minimalist nineties. In less than twenty-five years, the original steel and leather chairs that Mies van der Rohe designed for the 1929 Barcelona Pavilion — chairs that still embody most people's idea of "modern" — will officially be antiques. The old labels no longer apply.

But architects and decorators today seem unfazed by the challenge of synthesizing a few hundred years of history within the four walls of a living room. The best ones already know that the story of design is a very old one, that there is indeed very little new under the sun, and that everything is connected. And when you know what connects, say, a twentieth-century table by Eero Saarinen to a set of Victorian chairs, you can combine them with confidence.

Of course, trends in design are moving faster now than ever — partly because information travels so quickly in both print and cyberspace and partly because of the increasing influence of fashion. That world's insatiable hunger for recycling the recent past is reflected in the rather breathless homages that some young decorators are paying to twentieth-century decorating legends such as William Haines, Dorothy Draper, David Hicks, and the profession's reigning elder statesman, Albert Hadley — all of whom, ironically, made their reputations by digesting history and then making something new from it. The designers whose work is seen in this chapter have learned that lesson; their work respects the past as it embraces the present. After all, a theme park is a great place to visit, but you wouldn't want to live there.

POSH SPICE: MANHATTAN APARTMENT

Photographs by Vicente Wolf

We may be living in modern times, but most people's idea of luxurious living is stuck in another century: when we think of a grand New York apartment, visions of robber baron–style rooms, with red damask curtains and old master paintings, dance in our heads.

Well, not everyone's head. The owners of this Manhattan apartment hired the designer Vicente Wolf to take a typical Park Avenue apartment and turn it into something that was not a typical Park Avenue apartment. "They wanted something that had the sense of a glass of champagne," Wolf explains.

In one way, his job was easy: Wolf's clients collect large-scale contemporary art, hardly the stuff of stuffy rooms. But he resisted the impulse to design around the art; the last thing he wanted was something that looked more like a gallery than someone's home. "Those pieces aren't created in an austere environment," Wolf argues; hanging them in one "dehumanizes the art."

So Wolf infused these rooms with a humanism — albeit one of a decidedly posh variety — by carefully blending the old with the new. He transformed the apartment's architecture from what he called "sweetly traditional" to "thirties or forties glam" by replacing the old moldings with something a bit more severe, laying down a dark mahogany floor to contrast with the pale walls, and enlarging the doorway into the living room to exaggerate the room's scale. (He also made the dining room a bit smaller to make space for a guest room, since the apartment's second bedroom was turned into a library.)

In decorating the apartment, Wolf gave his clients the fizz they wanted by skillfully weaving antique and contemporary at every turn. In the living room, that meant surrounding a 1950s marble-topped table by Eero Saarinen with three nineteenth-century Italian side chairs and hanging a Venetian chandelier above it. The windows along one side of the living room are covered only with shades for a clean, modern feeling, while the windows at either end of the thirty-three-foot-long room are hung with voluminous silk curtains.

Similar curtains are hung all the way around the dining room, where they become undulating walls that serve as a backdrop for two big, colorful paintings by Eric Fischl and Ross Bleckner. Classic straight-backed upholstered chairs alternate with tapestry-covered 1940s chairs by the French designer Jules Leleu around an inlaid-wood table of Wolf's

Preceding page: In the center of the living room, an eighteenth-century Venetian chandelier and three nineteenth-century Italian chairs look right at home with a 1950s table by Eero Saarinen and a series of ink drawings by Brice Marden. The scale of the room, which is thirty-three feet long and twenty-three feet wide, is emphasized by the pale blue nineteenth-century Kirman rug, which runs the entire length of the room. Opposite page: Eric Fischl's painting *Offspring of a Murderous Love* hangs in the dining room, where Vicente Wolf lined the walls with silk curtains. Wolf designed the dining table, which is really four smaller tables that can seat eight people each, as well as the hanging lamps, wall sconces, and the mirrored standing sconce. "They bring light into the room without a chandelier," he explains. Above left: A geometric coffee table and classic upholstered seating illustrate the dialogue Wolf established between the traditional and the modern. Above right: Damien Hirst's painting *ABEI* presides over a pale blue velvet sofa, a low Chinese table, and a chair covered in cream buckskin.

design. In the master bedroom, a sleek wooden storage cube, also designed by Wolf, is tucked under a rather ornate eighteenth-century table.

This interplay continues all over the apartment. "Wherever there is something traditional, it's juxtaposed with something modern," Wolf says. "The openness of the space, the lack of pattern, and the pale blue-green color scheme are all very contemporary, so you know it's modern, but somehow it has a sense of the past."

Part of that sense comes from the sheer luxury of the materials Wolf uses here, such as silk and velvet, and even buckskin (in a nod to the French designer Jean-Michel Frank, a master at giving tradition a modern twist) to cover a chair. "Sixty percent of the things we do are sensory," Wolf explains. "You *feel* the quality of the paint job or the upholstery. That's what true luxury is to me."

But the lightness of these ample spaces and the wit with which Wolf balances past and present make these rooms fresh and young, which is just what his clients wanted. "In rooms like this, you're walking a fine line," the designer says. "If you go too much one way or the other, it can become predictable. And my clients are not predictable people."

Above: For the ample foyer, which is filled with more of the owners' collection of contemporary art, Wolf designed a console that brings to mind a massive library table. **Opposite page:** For the master bedroom, Wolf designed the bed — its headboard combines a traditional tufted headboard with more modern, tailored side panels. He also designed the sleek wooden storage cube that sits under an eighteenth-century French table and a trio of eighteenth-century Italian mirrors. The top of the table was covered in velvet and then overlaid with a thick piece of glass, to make the table user-friendly. As in the living room, the dominant color is a pale one — in this case, a delicate blue-green, or what Wolf calls a "seashore" palette.

THE GRAND TOUR:
WESTCHESTER COUNTY HOUSE

Photographs by Carlos Emilio

In the 1980s, Kevin Walz was well known for designing interiors and furniture that combined a tough, industrial chic with wit and charm. He and his wife, Barbra, a noted photographer who shot everything from fashion designers to icebergs, lived with their daughters, Jersey and Addison, in a Chelsea loft and a Victorian house on Shelter Island, knew Rolodexfuls of other famous creative types, and went to all the right parties. Life was, as Walz puts it, "huge."

But huge became overwhelming when Barbra died of cancer in 1990 and Walz was left to raise two children alone while running a six-person office and managing two households. "In the nick of time," Walz recalls, he won a fellowship at the American Academy in Rome, and in 1994 he and the girls left for the year abroad that would give him a new outlook on life. He's still there.

"As soon as I got here, life became really simple," Walz says. "Everything that was joyful — the inside of my head and my two kids — I brought with me." Pretty much everything else he got rid of. From his Roman base, Walz designs interiors and products for clients in Italy and New York. And over time, the centuries-old culture of Walz's adopted home has influenced his work. "There's a very different understanding of beauty and an appreciation of things that last over time," he explains. His signature approach became more expansive: the palette of materials and colors became richer and more varied; he mixes more old with the new.

A case in point: the interiors of this spacious, art-filled 1898 house in Westchester County, for which Walz "pulled from very different places and cultures" to find things "that resonated with our time yet represent their time." Thus, a nineteenth-century library table from Sri Lanka looks just right in the neoclassical entrance hall, and an eighteenth-century Genoese chandelier seems the perfect companion to one of Richard Diebenkorn's Ocean Park series paintings in the dining room.

The living room, which Walz wanted to look "more like a salon" than a formal living room, has a fairly neutral palette of colors and materials that defer to the colors in the art. A quirky assortment of twentieth-century furnishings mingles comfortably with Italian antiques, among others.

Walz took four years to design these interiors. "No one was in a hurry," he says, both of himself and of his extremely supportive clients. "We just wanted to make the right decisions."

But even without such leisurely timetables, the last decade has made Walz a more confident designer. As he says, "The choices I make are much nervier than the ones I would have made ten years ago."

Preceding page and opposite page: In the entrance hall, Kevin Walz uses furniture sparingly, but to striking effect. The Sri Lankan library table, which sits on a striped dhurrie rug, holds bronze busts by Judith Shea. **Above:** The entrance hall opens onto a porch that also serves as an outdoor living room. **Right:** One of Richard Diebenkorn's *Ocean Park* paintings is the focus of the dining room. An eighteenth-century Italian chandelier hangs above the table, which was designed by Walz and made by his brother, Barry. The top of the table consists of thin layers of cedar laminated with resin-impregnated fiberglass; it is strong but lightweight. Barry's expertise in canoe building was crucial to the success of Kevin's design, and both brothers delight in this kind of technological exploration.

Above: In the living room, an antique Sri Lankan child's bed serves as a bench in front of the fireplace. The room's eclectic furnishings include numerous twentieth-century pieces, such as the coffee table by Gio Ponti, that harmonize with the owners' sizable art collection. **Left:** A window seat in the master bedroom slopes to form a daybed. Walz's confident use of modernist furnishings against a turn-of-the-century architectural backdrop creates an appealing design dialogue. **Opposite page:** Walz designed the sweeping bronze bed and the elegant sofa, which sits under another painting by Diebenkorn. Against these relatively austere lines, the gilded and silk-upholstered nineteenth-century Italian bench strikes an opulent note.

COMPOUND INTEREST: WEISS HOUSE

OLDWICK, NEW JERSEY

Photographs by Scott Frances

at first glance, the white-shingled buildings shown here look as if they had settled into their lush green sur-roundings long ago. Only upon closer inspection can you see that while some of the structures are indeed very old, others are new. They owe their seamless integration to Steven Harris, a New York–based architect whose salient sty-listic trait is that he has none. Not that he doesn't have style; he just doesn't have *a* style.

You could visit an edgy downtown office for the actor John Leguizamo; a spare, New England–vernacular house in Connecticut; and a colorful, toylike house that jubilantly reflects its Florida beach-strip milieu — and never know that Harris designed them all. Which is fine with him.

"Basically, I'm distrustful of heroic, signature form making," he explains. "It leads to an architecture of commod-ity." Rather than going for a specific "look," Harris designs a house based on its setting and its owners' needs, which was just what he did for Claire and George David Weiss.

When the Weisses decided to turn their 1797 weekend house in Oldwick, New Jersey, into a year-round home, they wanted to enlarge and reconfigure it. Like many eighteenth-century houses, it was built too close to the road by today's standards. Moreover, visitors entered the property from the twentieth-century driveway and headed toward the side of the house — which meant, as Claire explains, "No one could find our front door."

In need of professional help, the Weisses began looking for an architect. In fact, they interviewed so many archi-tects, with such disappointing results, that they decided to sell the house. Then Harris materialized. "Steven was on our property for five minutes, maybe ten," says George, "and we knew we had our guy."

Harris's solution — which was so logical that no one had thought of it — was to build the addition perpendicular to the original house, so it and the new front door faced away from the road. Soon a new garage, a music studio for George (who has written such famous songs as "What a Wonderful World" and "Can't Help Falling in Love"), a dove-cote, a pool, and a pool house were also on the drawing board.

Working with the interior designer Lucien Rees-Roberts, who is the architect's longtime collaborator and com-panion, and Margie Ruddick, a Philadelphia landscape designer, Harris devised a sequence of buildings, lawns, and gardens that lead from the garage to the studio, past the dovecote, and across a flat, green lawn to the house and pool.

Preceding page: The new wing of the Weiss house overlooks a garden with a pergola. The new screened porch and kitchen behind it connect the new wing — which contains a living room and master bedroom — to the original 1797 house. **Above:** Opposite the new wing, Steven Harris added a two-story music studio (at left) and a towerlike dovecote. **Opposite page:** A tiny pool pavilion sits amid a bucolic landscape design by Margie Ruddick.

The beauty of the plan is that while the buildings are carefully arranged, they still have a casual, almost intimate feeling.

To Harris, the compound recalls traditional American farms, in that "there are no closed courtyards, no completely defined edges. There's always a missing side." (The property also includes a meadow that Ruddick transformed into a boxwood farm; it provides a cash crop that preserves the land's agricultural status for tax reasons.)

The house's interior has the rambling, cozy feel of a dwelling added to over time. The new wing, which contains a living-dining room downstairs and a master bedroom and bath upstairs, is joined to the old building (which now houses a library, office, and guest rooms) by a connecting structure that contains the kitchen and a screened porch. The new rooms were designed by Rees-Roberts in a modern nod to tradition; they are warm but clean lined, with simple, comfortable furnishings accented by Claire's growing collection of contemporary photography. "It's amazing how much she can get into something," says Rees-Roberts, who — like Harris and Ruddick — saw Claire as a collaborator more than as a client.

This mutual admiration society went on to collaborate on a house for the Weisses that overlooks the ocean in Cabo San Lucas, Mexico. Claire asked Harris to make this one modern, "kind of seventies, Hollywood glamorous," she says. Or, as she instructed Rees-Roberts, "Don't think beach house; think martini."

Top left: The new music studio and garage frame a view of the dovecote and the house's new wing beyond. **Bottom left:** In Claire Weiss's bathroom, a window above the industrial bathtub brings daylight in from another window beyond. The wall of violet Venetian mosaic tiles is punctuated by a rectangle of copper tiles. **Opposite page:** The living room is a showcase for Lucien Rees-Roberts's warm, low-key decorating, where modern pieces, such as the black wire Warren Platner tables, contrast with more traditional upholstered furniture. Since the original house was quite small in scale, Harris couldn't make the two-story addition too tall. In order to maximize the living room's height, Harris exposed the joists that support the floor above.

Left: The kitchen, which is part of the new construction, strikes a balance between tradition — with its wainscoting and double-hung windows — and modernity, with its stainless-steel cabinets and sleek light fixtures. A photograph by Tom Baril — part of Claire Weiss's collection of contemporary photography — hangs next to the corner fireplace. Above: The texture of the handmade glass inserts in the cabinet doors balances the coolness of the metal.

THE GREAT INDOORS:
BENTLEY-LaROSA HOUSE

BUCKS COUNTY, PENNSYLVANIA

Photographs by Scott Frances

t he famous admonition "Make no little plans," attributed to the architect Daniel Burnham, originally referred to cities. But lately it has become the rallying cry for weekend-house design. Looking at some of today's cottages-on-steroids, you're not sure whether you're seeing a rustic hideaway or a corporate conference center. So it is refreshing to see a weekend house that treads softly on the landscape, a feat that is all the more impressive when you consider that its owners are a pair of architects who make their living designing large and luxurious houses and apartments for clients with generous budgets.

Ronald Bentley and Salvatore LaRosa, two of the five partners in the New York firm B Five Studio, resisted the temptation to keep up with their well-heeled clients, although when they built the first phase of their rural retreat in Bucks County, Pennsylvania — a three-story tower — in 1987, they thought it might one day be the guest house for the "big house" they wanted to build up the hill on the sixteen-acre site, with its views of the Delaware River. "We were thirty-five," LaRosa recalls, laughing at his and Bentley's youthful ambition.

In the end, the two architects added a mere (by today's standards) twenty-four hundred square feet, in the form of a long, narrow, cedar-clad structure that connects to the tower with a short passageway. The addition, with its large expanses of glass, feels a bit like a railroad observation car — which makes sense when LaRosa explains that they placed the new building so that it glanced at the view the way you look out the window of a train, rather than faced it head on.

The addition has a living-dining room and LaRosa's studio on the main floor and the master bedroom and Bentley's studio on the floor below, which is dug into the hillside. (The kitchen, which connects to the living-dining area, is where it always was, on the main floor of the tower.) The spare furnishings, generous windows, and natural-toned finishes suggest an elegant treehouse — sheltering, yet at one with nature. There isn't even a front door; you just slide open a big window at the end of the walk from the parking court.

"Elegant" is a key concept here. For if the house's scope is modest, its execution is not. The architects' skill with materials and detail, a hallmark of their firm's work, is no less evident in this small house than it is in one of their clients' sprawling Park Avenue apartments. Custom mahogany windows, a massive indoor-outdoor fireplace made of local stone, and the thirteen-foot-long walnut refectory table with its X-shaped bronze base (in addition to some fine examples of twentieth-century modernist furniture) all attest to the architects' passion for balancing beauty and simplicity.

Still, they never let the architecture upstage its setting. "The place works on the level of detail and resolution," Bentley says, "but its connectedness to the outdoors allows you to ignore all the high-design aspects." Not that design hasn't found its way outdoors: the house's immediate landscape was carefully planned (by Douglas Reed of the landscape architecture firm Reed Hilderbrand Associates). A series of stone walls defines an outdoor living area and leads to a refreshingly secluded, luxuriously planted (by A. Billie Cohen) swimming pool. (Unlike many weekend-house owners, Bentley and LaRosa wisely opted to make Mother Nature the focus of the view, rather than the pool.)

The house, like the woods around it, continues to evolve. Its designers are in no hurry; their weekend work in progress is their idea of play. "Usually we get in and out of a project pretty fast," Bentley explains. "So this is different for us. We'll continue to develop it until we're too old to work here."

Preceding page: A thirteen-foot-long refectory table, made of walnut with x-shaped bronze supports, is one of the highlights of Ronald Bentley and Salvatore LaRosa's living room, a long, narrow space where vast expanses of glass offer sweeping views of the landscape, which includes the Delaware River. Left: The living room (with a glimpse of LaRosa's studio in the distance) has a massive double-sided stone fireplace. A large mahogany-framed window (at left) slides open in place of a front door. The dining chairs are by Jean Royère, and Marcel Wanders's famous Knotted Chair sits near the bronze coffee table and upholstered seating that LaRosa designed.

Above: LaRosa's studio, with its green-tinted plaster walls, is the most colorful room in the house and also the most eclectic: an antique Belgian bed coexists with twentieth-century pieces and custom bookcases designed by LaRosa. **Right:** A chest by Herbert Lippmann is topped by an Asian sword. **Opposite page:** A 1964 desk by Peder Pedersen for Vestergaard Jensen and a 1954 chair by Maurice Pré face a large skylit window, where a vintage Eames rocking chair offers a place to admire the view.

Above: The master bedroom, located a floor below the living room, features a one-of-a-kind headboard designed by Edward Wormley, who also designed the bedside tables. The bronze chair in the foreground belonged to its designer, Dan Johnson, and the carved bench at the foot of the bed is a South Sea Islands tribal piece. **Left:** The kitchen offers another spot from which to admire the landscape. **Opposite page:** A strikingly modern Spoon bathtub, designed by G. P. Benedini for Agape, occupies, as LaRosa says, "pride of place" in the master bathroom, with its limestone floors and views that rival those of any room in the house.

THE PERFECTIONIST:
APARICIO APARTMENT

NEW YORK

Photographs by William Waldron

f or Carlos Aparicio, design isn't just a profession; it's a passion. The Cuban-born architect, who grew up in Puerto Rico, was always fascinated by buildings. He even painted pictures of them as a child, much to the dismay of his mother's friends, who "told me to paint flowers for their living rooms," he recalls. As a student, first at the Rhode Island School of Design, and later at Harvard, Aparicio also learned as much about interior design and decorative arts as he did about contemporary architectural theory, thanks to his studies with Rodolfo Machado and Jorge Silvetti, Boston-based architects who know as much about antique furniture as they do about urban design and steel construction. This broad-based education is not typical of most architecture schools, which baffles Aparicio. "Architects have become less concerned with decorative arts, and that's a huge mistake," he says, adding that so many architect-designed interiors are "devoid of passion, inventiveness, and sophistication." On the other hand, Aparicio feels that his architectural training gives him an edge over many interior designers. "I'm just as comfortable discussing how stairs will be supported as I am talking to a client about fabrics."

One of Aparicio's early projects was the renovation of this Upper East Side apartment, where he lived for ten years. When he found it, it hadn't been renovated in decades and had what he calls a "slightly labyrinthine" floor plan. So the architect gutted the space and removed the corridors, creating a classical French enfilade of rooms that open directly into one another; the doors between them line up to create a vista from the nearest room to the farthest. Aparicio's office was the first room, and his bedroom the last, so far away that it didn't need to be separated by a corridor — although that didn't stop the architect from holding client meetings there. "There's a high level of intimacy when you're telling someone how to live," he says.

Moreover, the entire apartment functioned as a sort of design laboratory, where clients could see Aparicio's philosophy in action. For example, even though money was tight when he first started out, Aparicio insisted on coating the walls with Venetian plaster, a costlier surface than paint, because he believes that if a room doesn't have good bones, it doesn't matter how much you spend on the furniture. As he says, "If you are inviting people into your nest, you had better practice what you preach."

Preceding page: The understated luxury of French twentieth-century design is one of Carlos Aparicio's passions. A sycamore bookcase designed by André Arbus holds files and notebooks. A turn-of-the-century wood-and-metal ladder is elegant in its simplicity, and the parchment-and-metal light fixture was salvaged from a ballroom in the south of France. **Above left:** In the living room, a sofa designed by Aparicio is covered in raw silk. A silver-plated lamp by Gio Ponti sits on a table by Jean-Michel Frank, one of Aparicio's favorite designers. The painting is by Cindy Bennett. **Above right:** Adolphe Chanaux and Jean-Michel Frank designed the desk, which is made of limed oak and parchment. The lamp is by Maurice Lafaille. **Opposite page:** In the living room, an Austrian Biedermeier oval table stands near the window. Next to it is a pair of French Empire mahogany chairs, an 1850s Swedish bench, and an Italian mirror from the 1920s.

At the same time, Aparicio was starting to buy furniture — mostly from the twentieth century — in Europe, building an impressive collection that included a sycamore bookcase by André Arbus, a desk by Jean-Michel Frank, and animal-legged oak chairs by Marc du Plantier. Many of these pieces are interpretations of eighteenth-century designs (which Aparicio also loves), rendered in fine materials but with an austerity of form that made them truly modern. "I realized that I had an eye for furniture," he says, half kidding, "rather than the stock market, so I put all my money into furniture."

These pieces, and the ones that Aparicio now sells at BAC, his Manhattan gallery (he runs his architecture and interior design business there, too), share "a sense of my eye. I gravitate to clarity of ideas — something that looks logically put together but with an economy of means — very edited." And he likes to use furniture in similarly edited settings, as this apartment illustrates. "I like to leave room for furniture to breathe," Aparicio explains. "I don't like clutter. I like to take things away and put something better in their place."

Top left: The conference–dining room includes a French Arts and Crafts table in ebonized oak, 1940s French side chairs in limed oak, an early nineteenth-century velvet-upholstered oak bench, and a glass-and-chrome standing lamp by Jacques Adnet. A touch of Egypt comes through in the photograph, a print of the pyramids by Daniel Bibb. Bottom left: In the bedroom, a pair of 1940s oak chairs, upholstered in silk, by Marc du Plantier captured Aparicio's imagination with their "zoomorphic" legs; he says the chairs "look as if they are going to run away." The gilded metal standing lamp is by the French metalworking firm Baguès; its Greek-key design is "a very bold one, in the spirit of what Jean-Michel Frank would do," Aparicio says. Opposite page: The bed is covered in raw silk, one of Aparicio's favorite fabrics. The small ladder was designed by Alexandre-Gustave Eiffel, the designer of the Eiffel Tower. The ladder, says Aparicio, "is another kind of poetry." The room's stucco walls were designed by Aparicio and executed by Kenneth Widener, in three shades of a color the designer calls "limestone."

SUMMER CAMP: STERN HOUSE

LONG ISLAND

Photographs by Jason Schmidt

if the Rat Pack had hung out on Long Island instead of in Malibu or Palm Springs, this house might have been their headquarters. A glass living-dining pavilion with a massive stone fireplace offers dreamy views of the water. The mix of iconic midcentury modern furnishings with kitschy accessories and bold pattern, color, and texture recalls the days when the cool of the International Style gave way to a more exuberant, decorative school of modernism.

"It's *The Sandpiper* meets *North by Northwest*," says Jonathan Adler, the potter-turned-lifestyle-retailer who has added decorator to his curriculum vitae. The house, which is owned by Andrea Stern, a photographer whom Adler has known since college, embodies his particular brand of mod-crafty chic.

Originally designed in 1949 by Bertrand Goldberg (the architect of the Marina City apartment towers in Chicago), the house consisted of the glass pavilion plus kitchen and bedroom wings made from experimental prefabricated metal components. By the time Stern bought the house, it was in such bad shape that she essentially tore it down, leaving only the giant fireplace and a stone wall at the entry. David Schefer and Eve-Lynn Schoenstein of Schefer Design, a New York architecture firm, re-created the glass pavilion with a new kitchen, bedrooms, and family rooms that evoke the original design without copying it. "We wanted it to be a modern house, not a fifties house," Schefer says.

It is modern but playfully updated — as in the breakfast nook, whose leafy green fabric reminds Stern of her uncle's kitchen. Adler calls his client "very bold aesthetically," while Stern maintains that "the house would have looked very cold if we'd done a conventional modern interior." Adler's rooms, she adds, "pull from the past and make it very 'now.'"

Preceding page: Sculptural forms frame a view of the Stern house's pool terrace, which overlooks the water. **Above:** The master bedroom is decorated in bold geometric patterns — a Jonathan Adler hallmark — in pink and brown, which Adler calls "the chicest color scheme on earth." On the wall is Andrea Stern's photograph of her grandmother. **Left:** In the living room, a pair of Chinese-influenced love seats by James Mont sits on a camouflage-patterned rug designed by Adler; the vintage ceramic zebras are what he calls "very Palm Beach." Much of the metal in the house is brass or bronze, to harmonize with the architecture's honeyed palette — and because, Adler explains, "I am *so* postchrome."

Left: A pair of wicker basket chairs, purchased on the Internet, hangs against a backdrop of string curtains, which filter the light in the living room. Below: In the library, another of Andrea Stern's photographs hangs above a Paul Evans credenza. Sofas covered in a casual, shaggy cotton loop fabric contrast with more formal French-style armchairs. Opposite page: A stone wall, part of the original 1949 house, provides a rugged backdrop for two chairs by George Nakashima, an Albrizzi backgammon set, and a vintage cabinet with an overscale lamp by Adler, whose approach to the house plays off its macho-modern aesthetic.

Above: John-Paul Philippe painted the whimsical undersea mural in one of the bathrooms. Right: At night, the living room glows across the pool terrace. Adler discovered that an earlier, similar photograph of the house had been used in a magazine advertisement for Parliament cigarettes.

THE MAVERICKS

Much like any creative field, design is subject to the whims of fashion, peer pressure, and popular opinion. There's something comforting about being considered au courant; it's a kind of protective armor. But in design, as in other fields, there are also people who, as Henry David Thoreau said, hear a different drummer. And while it's fascinating to peek inside a dazzling contemporary weekend house or a grand, lavishly decorated apartment, there's something satisfying, in an entirely different way, about seeing someone's own aesthetic explored on a more down-to-earth, intimate scale. The houses and apartments that are illustrated in this section represent a number of design philosophies. But they have two important things in common: most were designed by the people who live in them, and they share a certain cheerful obliviousness to the outside world.

Granted, most of these elegant individualists design for a living, but they generally do so on a much larger scale. They make no pretense of living like their wealthy clients. Their expectations are more modest in scale (although not in execution), but what their homes lack in grandeur they more than make up for in ingenuity, quirkiness, and passion.

Many of these dwellings serve as laboratories for exploring ideas that might be too radical or idiosyncratic for a client but are essential to a designer's own evolution. And for anyone who is really interested in design, an architect or designer's own home usually offers the greatest insight into how that person's mind

and eye work. Of course, there are few designers who could exist without clients; design may be an art, but it is mostly a service profession, and a good designer gives clients a home that suits their lives and personalities, not his or her own. But still, there's something about that pure expression of someone's vision that inspires the designer in all of us. History is full of important examples: Thomas Jefferson's Monticello; Frank Lloyd Wright's Taliesin (the first one, in Spring Green, Wisconsin); the French decorator Madeleine Castaing's eccentric country house, the Manoir de Lèves; or Le Corbusier's tiny, modest, and tremendously moving vacation cabin overlooking the sea in the south of France, to name a few. These were designed to please no one but their owners and embodied everything they thought and felt about design. If they could do it, there's always the possibility that we can, too.

LE SHACK: CABANON

ROQUEBRUNE-CAP-MARTIN, FRANCE

Photographs by Jason Schmidt

When you hear the name Le Corbusier, you think of the sleek, white Villa Savoye or the chapel at Ronchamp, France, where the soaring roof seems to hover above massive walls. What you don't think of is a log cabin. A twelve-foot-by-twelve-foot one-room log cabin, no less. But in 1952, on a rocky hillside overlooking the Mediterranean in Roquebrune-Cap-Martin, France, the architect who was one of the godfathers of modernism built just that — a tiny retreat, called the Cabanon, to which he escaped as often as he could until his death thirteen years later.

Of course, this wasn't just any log cabin. Le Corbusier built the Cabanon both as a birthday present for his beloved (and, one suspects, long-suffering) wife, Yvonne, and as an experiment in a kind of minimal habitation. The architect, who at the time was working on plans for two vacation complexes in the area, wanted to see just how little space was needed for holiday living. Inspired by the compact design of ships' cabins and fascinated by the idea of monks' cells, he wrote of his idea: "Not a square centimeter wasted! A little cell at human scale where all functions were considered."

As he later recounted, Le Corbusier drew the plans for the Cabanon in forty-five minutes. "They were definitive," he said. "Nothing was changed." Designed according to the Modulor, his system of proportion that blended the golden section with a keen observation of human measurements, the cabin was a tightly orchestrated arrangement of built-ins, including a table-desk, bookcases, two beds, a wardrobe, a tiny sink, and a toilet in one corner of the room. Le Corbusier considered the toilet "one of the most beautiful objects industry has produced," so why hide it? (Yvonne — a former model who once jokingly said of the Paris apartment Le Corbusier designed for them, "All this light is killing me" — was used to this. When her husband insisted on installing the bidet near the bed in their apartment, she covered it with a tea towel.) There was no kitchen, because the architect took his meals at the Étoile de Mer, a tiny café next to which the Cabanon was built — on land Le Corbusier bought (in a trade for design services) from the café's proprietor, Thomas Rebutato, a onetime plumber. He and Le Corbusier had become friendly in 1949, when the architect was staying down the hill, at E.1027 (the now legendary villa that Eileen Gray had designed for Jean Badovici, an architect and publisher), and needed a place to feed his staff. The two men were so friendly, in fact, that Le Corbusier created a door that opened directly from his cabin into Rebutato's establishment, so that he could come and go without having to talk to anyone.

Preceding page: Inside Le Corbusier's Cabanon, built-in furnishings make the tiny interior more efficient. The remnants of a lamp sit on a shelf above the table that was designed for both work and dining. The window, with its partially mirrored shutters, frames a view of Monte Carlo in the distance. **Right:** A concealed door in the entrance hallway opens directly into the building that houses Thomas Rebutato's Étoile de Mer café, where Le Corbusier took all his meals. After repainting the hallway mural, the architect crossed out his signature and added another. **Opposite page:** On the other side of the wall, Le Corbusier painted another mural, in Thomas Rebutato's apartment behind the café. Rebutato, a former plumber, became a great friend of Le Corbusier's, and when the architect was building his cabin, Rebutato temporarily returned to his old trade.

The Cabanon's various pieces — the unmilled pine boards of the exterior, the plywood and oak interior, the walnut table, and even the chestnut front door — were prefabricated in Corsica and hauled to the rather remote site, which is still reachable only on foot. Small, square windows frame views of the sea and of Monte Carlo in the distance. Le Corbusier, who was also an accomplished artist, painted murals in the entrance hallway and on the bifold window shutters. Various accounts have both Charlotte Perriand, Le Corbusier's longtime collaborator, and the noted architect Jean Prouvé involved in the design of the furnishings.

Le Corbusier, who once said to Jerzy Soltan, an architect in his studio, "How nice it would be to die swimming toward the sun," did just that — in August 1965, less than two months short of his seventy-eighth birthday, when he suffered a heart attack in the water, not far from his cabin. (Yvonne had died in 1957.) In 1979 the Cabanon was acquired from the Fondation Le Corbusier by the Conservatoire du Littoral, an oceanfront land conservancy, which turned over the management of the cabin to the town of Roquebrune-Cap-Martin.

The Étoile de Mer has been closed for years but is perfectly preserved, and it is being donated to the conservancy by Thomas Rebutato's children (his son, Robert, was so enamored of Le Corbusier that he grew up to be an architect and is now the president of the association created for the preservation of the site). Ultimately, according to Renaud Barrès, an architect who is employed by Roquebrune-Cap-Martin as a sort of conservator of both the Cabanon and E.1027 (which the conservancy now owns, and which is under restoration), the two houses and the Étoile will be part of an architectural research center. "Modern architecture should be more than a museum," asserts Barrès, who was taken every summer as a child to the Cabanon by his architect father. Barrès's admirable sentiments notwithstanding, when the project is completed, this little stretch of Côte d'Azur hillside will become one of the most magnificent architectural pilgrimages in the world. To catch a glimpse into the lives of two of the twentieth century's greatest designers — and to be reminded that good things do come in small packages — is not only educational but also profoundly moving.

Above: Le Corbusier painted one panel of each window's bifold shutters. A photograph, curled with age, shows the architect's wife, Yvonne, and is tacked to the column that supports the sink on one side and contains storage on the other. **Opposite page:** The Cabanon, a historical landmark, sits in the shade of a carob tree. Its "log" exterior is actually made of unmilled pine boards. Inspired by the compact design of monks' cells and ships' cabins, and measuring a mere twelve feet by twelve feet, the cabin offered the architect the chance to prove how little space was actually needed for vacation living. It also afforded Le Corbusier a place to pursue his beloved pastime of swimming in the sea.

THE ENCHANTED COTTAGE:
SALASKY HOUSE

EAST HAMPTON, NEW YORK

Photographs by Scott Frances

if a designer's own house is a window into his psyche, it's a safe bet that Franklin Salasky has a rich inner life. The one-thousand-square-foot structure in East Hampton, New York, that Salasky — an architect and decorator, and a partner in the firm B Five Studio — calls his weekend home looks like a dollhouse on the outside. But once you step inside, you're in an enchanted cottage that, while cozy, seems improbably expansive. The official front door opens into an intimate, low-ceilinged dining area, with café curtains and a banquette. The fourteen-foot-high living room feels surprisingly grand for such a tiny house and contains a comfortable amalgam of furniture both stylish and mundane. The master bedroom is small enough to make the bed seem enormous by comparison, but the effect is like something from a children's book. (The guest room/study is even tinier, but its two windows flood it with sunlight.) The bathroom, which is housed in a former lean-to off the bedroom, is incongruously glamorous, with its iridescent bronze glass tiles and sunken tub. And nearly every door and window in the house looks out to trees and gardens. If there's one word that describes this place, it's *magical*.

But how it got to look this way has nothing to do with magic. When Salasky bought the little cottage more than a decade ago, it was in such dire shape that he had to build a new foundation and a basement and install new gas and water connections as well as a new heating system — never mind that it needed a new kitchen and bathroom. In case you're wondering what it was about this house that Salasky did like, it was the fact that the house sat on a quarter-acre lot that was behind another house and off to one side of the property, giving it what could be a very lovely and private yard. Even better were the site's mature trees. It was within his price range and in a part of the world not known for its real estate bargains. "I knew I couldn't find anything else like it, even though it needed a lot of work," Salasky recalls.

One of his major decisions was to move the driveway to allow more space for the garden, which Salasky, with the help of landscape designer Betsey Perrier, has filled with native plants. "I wanted the house to look settled in the landscape," he explains, "and I wanted to open the house to the landscape, to bring the outside in." He did this indoors by adding a high wainscot around the rooms, above which the walls are papered in various stylized botanical prints; the effect is that of vines creeping over the tops of fences. Salasky also opened the living room up to the screened

entrance porch with two pairs of bifold doors; when they are open, the room and the garden beyond seem to melt into one. "The view always goes back outside," he notes. And although every detail was carefully considered, the house never looks fussy or overdone.

Salasky calls it a very simple house, adding, "It's about reading, relaxing, gardening, and having friends around." The renovations took a lot more time and money than he expected them to; at the time, he recalls, "People thought I was nuts." But the results (and the fact that the house has appreciated greatly in value) proved the naysayers wrong. "Little did I know," he says, "that this would be the smartest decision I'd ever make."

Preceding page: Franklin Salasky ripped out the existing ceiling in his living room to give the intimate space a grand scale, and opened the room up to the screened porch beyond by adding two pairs of bifold doors. The curtain is an ethnic textile, and the eclectic furnishings include a Salasky-designed coffee table and an Ingo Maurer chandelier. **Above:** In the master bedroom, Salasky used a chalky green casein paint on the four-poster bed. The wallpapers — a wood grain and a stylized leaf pattern — typify Salasky's bring-the-outdoors-in approach to decorating the house. **Opposite page:** A view from the living room, through the bedroom, into the master bathroom.

Above: The master bathroom combines rugged plywood walls with a more refined floor of iridescent glass tiles and an old-fashioned Dutch door that frames a garden view. **Left:** Salasky's abundant, romantic garden was designed in collaboration with the landscape designer Betsey Perrier. "I wanted the house to look settled in the landscape," he says.

Top right: The kitchen (with the dining area beyond) mixes traditional linoleum flooring and off-white tiles, vintage decorative accessories, and up-to-the-minute appliances. **Bottom right:** A door in the master bedroom opens onto a small terrace, shaded by a pergola, in the middle of the garden behind the house. **Opposite page:** The low-ceilinged dining area is made even more intimate by the addition of a banquette and café curtains. To make the banquette, Salasky simply put a door on concrete-block legs and placed a futon atop the door. Gio Ponti's iconic Superleggera chairs flank a table designed by Salasky.

BLOCK ISLANDS: JAYNE-ELLIS LOFT

NEW YORK

Photographs by William Waldron

making a loft livable — that is, bringing it down to human scale — is a problem that designers have tried to solve with everything from modernist sliding steel-and-glass walls to Georgian doorways. But Thomas Jayne, a New York decorator, took a route that redefines the phrase "economy of means." With just four colors of paint, Jayne transformed the two-thousand-square-foot SoHo loft that he shares with Rick Ellis, a food stylist and culinary historian, into a series of welcoming "virtual rooms."

When they bought the loft, they knew that their building was soon to undergo major renovations, so Jayne and Ellis decided to postpone work on their own space until the construction was completed. In the meantime, they moved in only a minimum of their many possessions (which include antique furniture and decorative objects accumulated by the extremely knowledgeable Jayne, and Ellis's five thousand books on American cookery) so that they wouldn't have to move them out again when their own renovations began. Alas, their well-edited selection of furnishings — even the massive Victorian bed that belonged to Jayne's great-great-grandparents — practically disappeared in the loft's vast white space. "I was dwarfed," admits Jayne, who, at six feet seven, towers over most people.

But he knew what to do. Much of his work, as Jayne explains it, is "about organizing spaces with color, as they did in the eighteenth and nineteenth centuries." But his approach to the loft also recalls the way twentieth-century designers like Charles and Ray Eames used color as floating planes. Jayne applied big rectangles of blue, green, pink, and ocher to the walls to define the dining and living areas in the main space and to make the fourteen-foot-high walls relate to the scale of the furniture in all the rooms. (Even in the bedroom, Jayne added two color blocks to make the massive bed seem, well, more massive.)

Jayne's palette included colors, such as bubble gum pink and acid green, "that aren't necessarily used in polite decorating," he says. "But we knew we weren't going to live with it forever. Why be tasteful?"

Preceding page: A pink rectangle painted on the white wall defines the dining area in Thomas Jayne and Rick Ellis's loft, and serves as a backdrop for portraits of Jayne (right) and Ellis (left) by John Woodrow Kelly. **Left:** Rectangles of blue and pink define the living area, where antique English side chairs flank a copy of Houdon's bust of Benjamin Franklin, which is adorned with a Mason's hat. The gilded standing lamps on either side of the nineteenth-century sideboard are by the twentieth-century designer Diego Giacometti. **Below:** An ocher-colored block frames the bed, which is a Jayne family heirloom. An identical ocher block frames a chest of drawers on the opposite wall. Jayne bought the oval mirror at the Pottery Barn and painted it coral.

Above: An acid-green block defines one end of the dining area. Sconces by the British designer Belinda Eade flank a pink nude by Van Jensen, which Jayne and Ellis bought in the East Village. The shield-back chairs on either side of the antique American drop-leaf table are eighteenth century; their faux-tortoise finish was added sometime later. Opposite page: The massive Victorian bed belonged to Jayne's great-great-grandparents and has been the designer's since childhood. The blocks of color on the walls help to mediate between the scale of the furnishings and the loft's fourteen-foot-high walls.

SMALL WONDER:
SLESIN-STEINBERG HOUSE

SAG HARBOR, NEW YORK

Photographs by Marie-Pierre Morel

for Suzanne Slesin and Michael Steinberg, design isn't just a casual interest; it's more a way of life. Slesin, a writer and editor who is the author or coauthor of a number of influential design books, including the iconic volume *High-Tech,* has been taking the pulse of the design world for years. Steinberg, who is now an art dealer, used to own Furniture of the Twentieth Century, one of the more influential modern-design showrooms of the 1980s. The couple has been collecting examples of classic modern and contemporary design for twenty-five years, but when they chose to sell their weekend house on Long Island and buy another, Slesin and Steinberg decided that less, as Mies van der Rohe said, is indeed more. They downsized, to a twelve-hundred-square-foot house on three acres in Sag Harbor, and hired the designer Michael Formica (with James Orsi) to renovate the building, which had originally been a shed. "We wanted to turn it into a luxurious but interesting hotel suite," Slesin recalls. "We didn't want to feel guilty if we didn't go there every weekend."

Given the house's small size — the structure measures a mere thirty by forty feet — Formica chose to keep things simple. "It was about dividing the space in a logical way," he explains. "I love the idea of a central core of utilities." An open, central kitchen is located back-to-back with a bathroom that is almost extravagantly large for a house this compact but that allowed Formica — his name, unlike that of the surfacing material, is pronounced with the accent on the first syllable — to hide all the mechanical elements in a space above its ceiling. On either side is a bedroom and guest room/study, both of which are separated from the main living space only by sliding screens; the bathroom is the only room with a real door. "Only good friends can stay here," Slesin quips. There isn't even a proper front door; a wall of hinged glass doors lets you in. But the house's lack of formality is perfectly suited to its use as a weekend getaway. "What most people respond to is how welcoming it feels," says Steinberg. The couple gives Formica's design much of the credit for making such a small house so luxurious. "Michael's spatial concept gave it . . . style," says Slesin. "Not purely function," adds Steinberg.

The house is furnished with a carefully edited selection of the couple's favorite things. A pair of Florence Knoll tables and two chairs by Pierre Jeanneret exemplify midcentury modernism, while newer pieces, like the daybeds by the sculptor Rachel Whiteread, the provocative chest of drawers by Tejo Remy for Droog Design, and the table by the artist Do-Ho Suh, with thousands of tiny plastic figures under its glass top, represent the contemporary outlook that fascinates Steinberg — but that, Slesin says, she also loves. Slesin's own sensibility is more eclectic, which is why

she's grateful that the property came with two tiny cabins that had once belonged to a roadside motel. In them she stores what she calls "my folk art," the pieces that didn't fit in with the main house's pared-down aesthetic.

Still, this house's brand of modernism is very forgiving. "If it were really modern, it would have been furnished with a much more limited palette," notes Slesin. "I could never be a minimalist."

Preceding page: The open kitchen (with the living area in the foreground and the dining area beyond) is the center of Suzanne Slesin and Michael Steinberg's weekend house. **Above:** The house has no front door — only a series of sliding doors. **Right:** The deck offers views of a meadow and the two tiny cabins (which had once belonged to a roadside motel) that Slesin uses to store treasured objects that don't quite mesh with the house's more pared-down aesthetic. **Opposite page:** In the guest room–study, daybeds designed by the British artist Rachel Whiteread are among the many objects in the house that blur the lines between art and design.

Top left: A tub designed by Philippe Starck is the centerpiece of the bathroom, which also contains items such as the flower-shaped mirror by the artist Jeff Koons and the well-known S-Chair by British designer Tom Dixon. **Bottom left:** The comfortable living area includes a traditional sofa, vintage twentieth-century armchairs by Pierre Jeanneret (the brother of Le Corbusier), and contemporary pieces such as the Garouste and Bonetti rug and the recycled-wood Favela chair, which was designed by Fernando and Humberto Campana. **Opposite page:** In the living area, shelves hold twentieth-century wooden glove forms and twentieth-century objects in wood — such as the Dansk wooden ice bucket — and spun aluminum. Two figures by Kasimir Malevich sit on the wood table, which (like the chairs) was designed by Alvar Aalto.

Below: In the master bedroom, Tejo Remy's chest of drawers, designed for the Dutch collective Droog Design, is made of twenty separate drawers that are held together by a mover's strap. Slesin says that the piece "always makes me smile and embodies everything that appeals to me about design — it's quirky, folksy, partly recycled, thought provoking, and not pretentious."
Opposite page: The bedroom, like the guest room, is separated from the house's main living areas by sliding screens; only the bathroom has a real door. The unpainted plywood ceilings add to the house's casual air. In the foreground, the dining table, by the Korean artist Do-Ho Suh, features thousands of plastic figurines under its glass top. Steinberg notes that "people are fascinated by it. They really react to its fresh sculptural expression and the obsessiveness of the artist." Slesin and Steinberg commissioned the table after seeing similar figures in one of the artist's gallery installations.

THE RED AND THE BLACK:
MCKAY-D'ARMINIO APARTMENT

NEW YORK

Photographs by Jason Schmidt

a s any decorator will tell you, tiny rooms are no place for the timid. Jeff McKay isn't a decorator; he had his own advertising agency for ten years before he quit to smell the roses. But he has a keen eye, and he's no stranger to small spaces. (He gave his previous apartment — all 310 square feet of it — extra punch by painting it six shades of silver.) So when faced with decorating a small Manhattan pied-à-terre for himself and his partner, Michael D'Arminio, McKay thought big.

Since the six-hundred-square-foot studio is really just a place to sleep, and because he can't sleep without windows, McKay put an antique brass canopy bed smack in the middle of the room, while turning the windowless sleeping alcove into a dining/work space, adorned with decorative objets perched on brackets, in the manner of an eighteenth-century salon. At the foot of the bed is a sitting area with a settee and two plush chairs, and in the kitchen, which is seldom used for cooking, McKay added a silver-gilt bench, an art deco bar cabinet, and an elegant mirror over the sink. As he says, "Doing dishes is boring, so you might as well check your hair."

The prevailing aesthetic is boho eclectic — your great-aunt Fanny meets the Rat Pack — but with a pronounced French accent.

Why French? Because Paris is where D'Arminio, a brand-imaging consultant in the fashion and beauty industries, is based and where McKay spends much of the year. And it was there, in a "very glamorous" Napoléon III–era apartment that the couple lived in for three years, that McKay learned to love *le style français*. "Everything is symmetrical there," he says admiringly. "If they have to put in a door, they put in a false second door to balance it."

Not so back in Manhattan, where virtually nothing in the studio was symmetrical; the closer McKay looked, the more imperfections he saw. But the New York apartment is a rental, so rather than invest a lot of money in correcting its shortcomings, McKay — having learned a valuable lesson in French chic — decided simply to camouflage them.

"I painted everything that wasn't symmetrical black," he explains. In fact, he painted the apartment's east and west walls black and the north and south walls (as well as the floor) white. Then, with the help of James Corbett, a friend who is an interior designer, McKay added touches that were literally French, such as the photomural of an interior at Versailles and the gilt Baguès side table. There were also the frankly faux, like the French provincial–style settee and the inexpensive brackets that McKay painted himself to display tchotchkes ranging from vintage Venini glass to the Lucite clock that once sat on his grandmother's television.

McKay calls the result "a Walt Disney version of France," which is not so far from the truth. He has, after all, turned an uninspired space into a magic kingdom.

Preceding page: A view into the main living-sleeping area of Jeff McKay and Michael D'Arminio's pied-à-terre, with the dining alcove at left. **Above:** A red lacquer Chinese cabinet stands out against a black wall in the main room, while the effect is reversed in the kitchen beyond. **Below:** The wall behind the bed is covered with a photomural — made from a vintage postcard of Versailles — that is intended to expand the space visually. **Opposite page:** The sitting area, at the foot of the bed, features an eclectic array of furnishings, including a Bugatti shelf, twentieth-century tub chairs, and a Chinese lacquer baby bath that is used as a coffee table. The rug is a custom design.

Top left: An elegant mirror adds an incongruous but stylish touch to the apartment's tiny kitchen. Bottom left: The bathroom is vintage New York, with its black-and-white checkerboard tile floor and white tiles on the wall. Black walls and leopard-print towels add zing. Opposite page: The apartment's sleeping alcove was turned into a dining room. McKay bought inexpensive decorative brackets, painted them black and white, and turned them into striking display elements. The table is made of a standard-issue restaurant-supply base and a mirrored top, but the chairs are vintage Hans Wegner.

CAESAR'S OTHER PALACE:
BARATTA APARTMENT

NEW YORK

Photographs by Jason Schmidt

his mother cringed. His friends were horrified. And many visitors were flabbergasted at first, even if they warmed up to it later. But Anthony Baratta doesn't care. It's his apartment and he'll overdecorate it if he wants to.

In this cozy Greenwich Village one-bedroom, costly nineteenth-century plaster casts of classical nudes vie for attention with clearly camp table lamps, while plaid clashes cheerfully with leopard, and hot colors throb in counterpoint to graphic black and white. Never mind that Baratta and his business partner, William Diamond, are already famous in the design world for their fearless mixtures of colors, patterns, and periods. Baratta had wanted to walk on the still wilder side. "I wanted to go beyond taste," he explains.

He also went beyond kitsch.

Sure, it's easy to spot the references to Las Vegas high-roller suites, Carnaby Street, and the Miami Beach hotels by the legendary architect Morris Lapidus. Less obvious are the influences of Baratta's own grounding in art history and design and of his decorating heroes, such as Billy Baldwin (rooms designed for easy conversation), Sister Parish (unorthodox combinations of color and pattern), and Michael Taylor (bold use of large-scale furniture). Baratta's grasp of proportion, his eye for quality, and his knack for transforming something tacky (he reupholstered a white vinyl ottoman from the 1960s) into something sumptuous (he chose white leather) made a tour de force of what might otherwise carry a big "Don't try this at home" warning. But for Baratta, skating on the edge is exactly the point. "I'm not interested in 'pure' style," he insists. It's all in the mix.

Preceding page: A view from the foyer of Anthony Baratta's apartment into the living room; the giant-scaled plaid carpet offers a clue that this is no ordinary interior. **Above:** In the living room, Baratta's confident decorating mixes the improbable: plaid with leopard, classicism (the male nude and the giant foot) with camp (the harlequin lamp), against a backdrop of bold color. **Opposite page:** A Victorian settee, transformed by large-scale harlequin-patterned upholstery, is juxtaposed against a 1960s op-art-patterned lacquered cube and a 1950s-style terrazzo coffee table that Baratta designed himself, as well as the classical imagery on the walls and the folding screen.

Top left: Baratta covered the bedroom walls in an eye-popping magenta wool felt, the better to contrast with the apple-green silk satin that he used for the gilded baroque-style headboard and monogrammed bedspread. Bottom left: For a folding screen in the bedroom, Baratta recolored the famous wallpaper, adorned with leaping zebras, that lines the walls at Gino's, the legendary Italian restaurant in Manhattan. The brass lamp next to the bed was chosen more for its heroic scale than for its design pedigree. The plaid fabric on the tubular steel chair is also used for the room's curtains. Opposite page: The foyer's Regency-style striped tent serves as a foil for the zebra-covered twentieth-century chair by Guglielmo Ulrich and the gilded sunburst mirror, along with yet another classical figure.

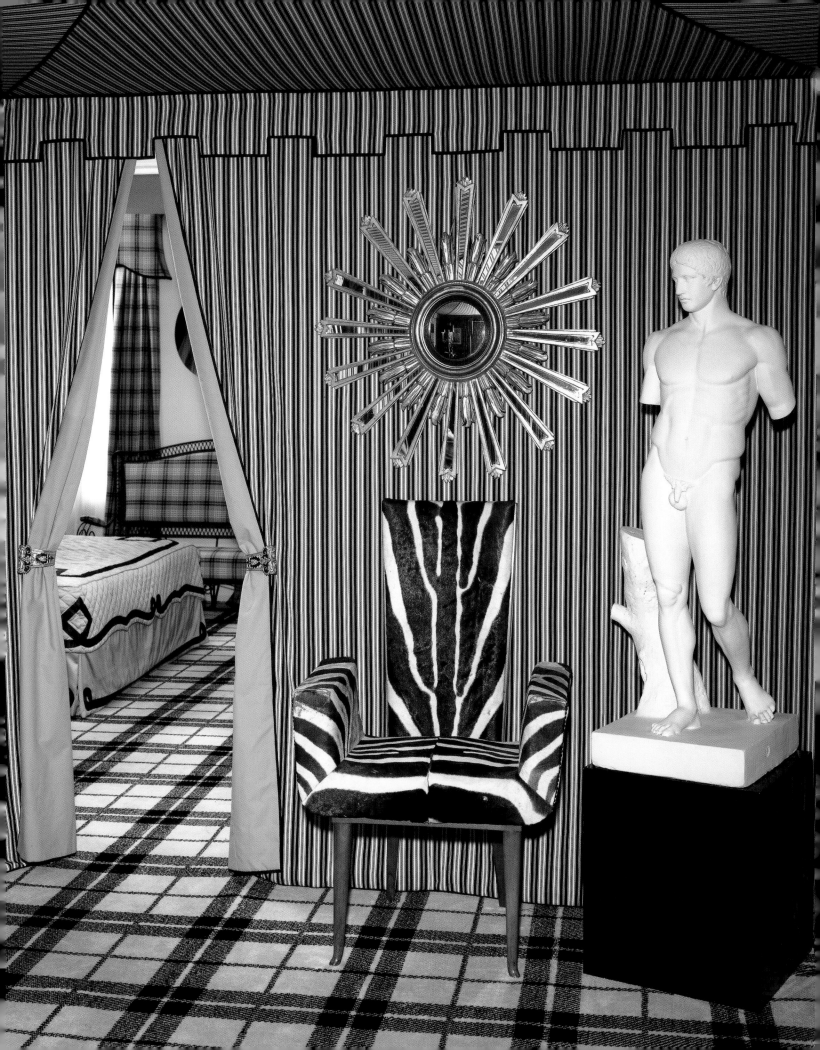

FLOATS LIKE A BUTTERFLY:
BARATTA APARTMENT

MIAMI BEACH

Photographs by Jason Schmidt

i n the world of decorating, it's common knowledge that Anthony Baratta fears no color. He and his business partner, William Diamond, are known for their liberal use of color and pattern — think giant plaids or harlequin prints — in rooms that are lively without feeling busy. Baratta himself once lived in a New York apartment that was a skillfully controlled riot of warm, saturated hues like apple green and bright orange. But for this Miami Beach pad, Baratta — in collaboration with Diamond — turned his genius for color in a lighter, breezier direction. The clashing patterns, abrupt scale changes, and juxtapositions of old and new are still there — but this time, in a resort-wear version.

Baratta's tropical pied-à-terre was the product of one of life's more stressful changes — the breakup of a relationship. The designer had planned to spend Christmas that year in St. Barthélemy, but when he discovered that his now ex-beau was booked into the same hotel, he needed a plan B. "You can't fit two Napoléons on one Elba," Baratta quips.

So, on the theory that living well is the best revenge, Baratta got back the hefty deposit he had made on his St. Barts lodgings and put it toward the purchase of a small (one-thousand-square-foot) two-bedroom apartment in a 1930s building just outside Miami Beach's historic art deco district. "The apartment had higher ceilings than many others in the building, concrete floors, deco pilasters, and corner windows," explains Baratta. "I knew that with a coat of white paint, it would be great."

White paint? No, Baratta wasn't going minimalist on us, but his initial decorating scheme produced a graphic black-and-white look. Then he brought in two hot pink bougainvillea plants for a party, and when a friend from the fashion world saw them and said, "I get it! Black and white with color as an accent. You use color like a handbag," Baratta took the hint and added more color — including a captivating wallpaper in a butterfly pattern by Rob Wynne, a New York artist.

The addition came not a moment too soon, if you ask Diamond. "I always said to Tony, 'Black and white with color,'" he recalls. "Color is what makes black and white black and white," he adds, in a pronouncement worthy of Diana Vreeland. The main accents — hot pink and turquoise — were taken from the canvas fabric that Baratta used as a background for the oversize monograms on the living room's two Victorian sofas. "Those were the colors that won," the designer explains.

In keeping with South Beach's permanent-vacation gestalt, Baratta's decorating was much looser and more casual here than in New York. Indeed, many of the apartment's furnishings came out of the designers' own storage rooms. Diamond laughingly describes them as a collection of "the rejects, mistakes, and disasters from all our other projects."

For instance, the elegant Napoléon III faux-bamboo folding settee and chairs were spotted by the designers nearly

Preceding page: In the bedroom of Anthony Baratta's Miami Beach apartment, an elegant Napoléon III faux-bamboo folding settee looks right at home with the Victorian painted-metal-and-brass bed, against the whimsical backdrop of artist Rob Wynne's butterfly-patterned wallpaper. The wide-striped fabric on the chair is a typical Diamond Baratta touch; the bed pillow is covered with a Hermès beach towel. **Above left:** The living room combines a Victorian sofa, covered in another wide-striped fabric, with 1930s French armchairs and a coffee table that is actually a high-impact plastic shipping case for a drum. **Above right:** The hot pink of the monogrammed oval in the sofa is one of the accent colors in the apartment's mostly black-and-white color scheme. **Opposite page:** The photograph of the old car that hangs above the dining table is from *Girls in Cuba,* a 1998 photojournal by Gianni Giulianelli.

twenty years ago. The Victorian sofas in the living room were a "mistake" too, albeit someone else's. The designers found them languishing in the basement of one of New York's top upholsterers, who had made them for "a famous decorator who couldn't pay the bill." And the French 1930s chairs (with their original leather upholstery) were irresistible at two hundred dollars apiece, but they had no seat cushions. Baratta soon remedied this situation by creating new ones out of sheepskin.

Still, this assortment of "rejects" is pretty high toned, so Baratta added some downright ordinary touches — with, of course, far from ordinary results. Next to the very good English Victorian brass-and-painted-metal bed, he made a

striking storage unit out of a stack of musical instrument cases — sort of a rock-star take on 1980s high tech. And around the dining table, Baratta placed a group of humble wood-and-canvas director's chairs. "To me, they're as good as Le Corbusier cube chairs," he asserts, referring to the pricey tubular steel chairs with boxy leather cushions that are a modernist icon.

Baratta's Florida home away from home turned out to be a diversion as well as a retreat. "I have a wonderful life, but sometimes it gets pretty complicated. I wanted to be able to lose myself in this place, and when I walk in the door, I feel as if I'm floating in light, just like one of the butterflies on the wall."

MODERN LIVING

My first, thrilling exposure to modern architecture was a visit, in the early 1960s, to the Monsanto House of the Future at Disneyland. Its cantilevered structure, which was enclosed by curving plastic walls, contained a vision of domestic ease and efficiency, of better living through technological innovation and synthetic materials. (The house was built by the Monsanto Chemical Company and designed by architects from the Massachusetts Institute of Technology.) The house wouldn't rank with the great wonders of modernist architecture, but I'm convinced that it sparked my lifelong enthusiasm for all things modern. Some of its marvels, like a microwave oven and big-screen television, would come to be commonplace in today's houses, and its vision of plastic furniture is being more readily (albeit selectively) adopted by consumers, but its architecture was more of a curiosity than a revelation to most of the twenty million people who saw it in the ten years (1957–1967) of its existence. Such has seemed the fate of the modernist house in our culture. The popular perception of modern architecture is that it is cold and unfriendly. And while there is ample evidence to bolster that view, there are just as many examples to the contrary — depending, in large part, on the skill of the architects and designers in question. As in any creative endeavor, there are many followers but only a few leaders.

The seven houses and one apartment shown in this chapter represent only a few examples of contemporary domestic architecture that have been published in *The New York Times Magazine*. They are all descended, however indirectly, from the work of the great architectural pioneers of the twentieth century —masters such as Frank Lloyd Wright, Mies van der Rohe, and Le Corbusier. The modernist movement sought to free architecture from the strictures of formalist tradition and to embrace modern materials and technologies in order to allow people to live and work in environments that reflected the ever-advancing progress of the machine age. But not everyone shared the movement's utopian zeal; Wright's visionary work, for example, was alternately revered and reviled. Apart from a few notable examples such as the Case Study House program or the communities of Eichler Homes, modernist architecture never even got close to the American mainstream.

Today the machine age has given way to the electronic age, and while architects in the twenty-first century are experimenting with forms and materials that are innovative for our time, modern domestic architecture remains a specialty; historically inspired styles still rule the housing marketplace. Nevertheless, a growing number of architects and designers are exploring those ideas that shaped modernism in the first place: the clear expression of structure; open, flowing spaces; and an intimate relationship between indoors and outdoors. The dwellings shown here are made with materials that range from costly to off-the-shelf, but they share an elegant serenity, and they exemplify just how livable modern architecture can be.

A LABOR OF LOVE: VILLA PLANCHART

CARACAS, VENEZUELA

Photographs by Jason Schmidt

On a hilltop in Caracas, Venezuela, overlooking the city and the mountains that surround it, sits one of the postwar era's most exuberant works of domestic architecture. The Villa Planchart was designed for Armando and Anala Planchart by the Italian architect Gio Ponti (1891–1979) and completed in 1956. Ponti designed not only the ten-thousand-square-foot, six-bedroom house but all the furniture and many of the objects within it with the spirit and sensuality that were the hallmarks of his humanistic brand of modernism. Still occupied by Anala Planchart, the house is a testament not just to a couple's happy marriage but also to an enduring friendship between clients and architect.

By the early 1950s, Armando Planchart was a successful General Motors dealer in Venezuela. He and Anala had been married since 1936. "My husband was a very unusual man," she says. "His first priority in life was to make me happy. In forty-two years, we never spent a night apart."

The couple had no children, and Armando Planchart, having decided that it was time to enjoy the fruits of his labors, told his wife that he wanted to buy a farm. She didn't. "One day," she explains, "I was driving around, and I saw this land. So I told my husband that I had found a beautiful 'farm.' 'In Caracas?' he replied. But one day he said, 'Get dressed, I'm going to take you someplace.' We came here, and he had a table, champagne, and caviar in the trunk of the car. And he said to me, 'It's yours. What are you going to do with it?' "

The Plancharts found the answer in the pages of *Domus,* the architecture and design magazine that was founded by Ponti in 1928 (and still exists). They liked what they saw of his work in the magazine and flew to Milan to interview the architect, who designed everything from office buildings (he would soon design his famous Pirelli tower in Milan) to ship interiors (such as that of the *Andrea Doria*) to chairs and teacups with the same intelligence and elegance.

One thing that struck Anala Planchart immediately was Ponti's willingness to listen to their opinions. "He wasn't the kind of architect who said, 'I'm going to do this,' " she explains. When Ponti did a preliminary sketch of a house that evoked a hacienda, she said, "That's a Spanish house. I want a modern house." When asked what else she wanted, Anala Planchart replied, "no walls," referring to an open, expansive interior. Her husband, an amateur orchid grower, wanted plants throughout the house.

Preceding page: For the Villa Planchart's formal dining room, its architect, Gio Ponti, designed tables — with enameled, geometric-patterned tops — that could stand alone or be grouped together for large gatherings and could adjust from coffee-table to dining height. Above: The roof of the house seems to hover just above the structure. Ponti told the Plancharts that their house would look like a butterfly that had alighted on a mountain. Opposite page: The airy, orchid-filled living room abounds with Ponti-designed furniture, still covered in its original leather upholstery. A television room above can be closed off with pivoting panels.

By 1954 Ponti had made his first trip to the Plancharts' hilltop site and pronounced that their house would look like a butterfly that had alighted on a mountain.

The finished product may not look exactly like a butterfly, but you could say that it floats like one. The mosaic-tile-covered sides of the house don't quite meet at the corners, and the roof appears to hover just a few inches above the building. Inside, the main living area is a soaring, double-height space filled with color, light, and flowers; it opens onto a junglelike courtyard and also leads to a spectacular dining room, where a tall window frames a cinematic view of the city and mountains. Ponti layered tone on tone and pattern on pattern: the floors are a crazy-quilt

assemblage of big marble slabs in various colors; the ceilings are diagonally striped in yellow and white; and the dining room tables are enameled with geometric designs in luscious shades of blue, green, yellow, and pink. In the hands of a lesser talent, this joyful visual noise would have been a cacophony.

Ponti's seemingly inexhaustible ingenuity produced wonderful surprises: In the bedrooms, the headboards ("organized walls," he called them) have built-in reading lights, cigarette lighters, and ashtrays (he had first seen them on a train). The glass-fronted closet doors double as a photograph album to record the Plancharts' life together, and ingenious, electric-powered cabinets in the study

revolve to either display or conceal Armando Planchart's collection of hunting trophies. (This was Ponti's solution to the one disagreement he had with his clients — he disliked the animal heads.) Custom-designed dinner plates bear one of Ponti's drawings of the house in gold. And the rooms are filled with various iterations of the lightweight wooden chair that Ponti designed for the Italian manufacturer Cassina, which culminated in the "Superleggera" (Italian for *superlight*) chair of 1957 — you can pick it up with one finger.

Long after the house was completed, the Plancharts remained close to Ponti and his wife, Giulia. (She died in 1975, followed by Armando Planchart in 1978 and Ponti himself in 1979.) Anala Planchart, the lone surviving member of this mutual admiration society, takes what she calls a "panoramic view" of life, but her home is still a priority: "I like the house to be alive," she insists. That is why, before Armando Planchart died, the couple established a foundation to maintain the house. They had the foresight not only to hire a modern architect but also to ensure that his visionary design wouldn't be lost to history.

Above: In the study, cabinets open and close electrically in order to display — or hide — Armando Planchart's collection of hunting trophies. (Ponti himself preferred to hide them.) The display cases swivel closed behind enameled panels. Ponti designed the biomorphic-looking Round chair at right, and he created the Mariposa armchairs for the Italian manufacturer Cassina in the 1950s. **Opposite page:** Another wall in the study contains a vintage built-in television, and shelves house a collection of enameled copper objects that Ponti designed for De Poli and that, like everything designed by the architect, have become highly collectible.

Top left: On one of the dining room tables is a plate from one of several china services that Ponti designed for the Plancharts; this one features their house illustrated in gold. The silver flatware was designed by Ponti for Reed & Barton. Top right: Ponti designed four open-air porches for the house, all of which were carved out of the building. They have the same marble floors as the interiors, dissolving the distinction between inside and outside. Against this porch's stone-mosaic wall stands Ponti's 1957 black-and-white Superleggera chair; it was designed with a mate in which the colors were reversed. Right: A staircase leads from the living room down to the basement-level playroom. The stair risers are faced with various kinds of marble; the handrail was custom-made to display part of the Plancharts' mineral collection. The chairs, originally designed by Ponti in 1950 for Fornasetti, are wrapped in newspapers chosen by Armando Planchart. Opposite page: The Plancharts commissioned a large wall piece from Fausto Melotti, a frequent Ponti collaborator, for the stairwell off the living room. Melotti also designed the tiles for several of the house's bathrooms.

SKY BOX: WEEKEND HOUSE

LONG ISLAND

Photographs by Nikolas Koenig

this is neither the most humble house to be built on Long Island's east end nor the most lavish. At four thousand square feet, it's hardly a shack, yet it would fit neatly into a wing of some of its more gargantuan neighbors. There is also a guest house that measures eleven hundred square feet, which meets the bare minimum required by building codes, and a pool with an outdoor dining terrace. Each of these elements — main house, guest house, and pool — is simple but elegant and set so discreetly into the wooded site that you can't see one from another. Even though it encompasses fifteen acres, you might call this an anti-estate.

David Piscuskas of 1100 Architect said that he and his partner, Juergen Riehm, wanted to design something "straightforward but beautiful" that minimally intruded on its surroundings while offering a view of them. And since their clients did not have a limitless budget, the architects had to decide where to scrimp and where to spend. Their solution was to make the main house a three-story stack of boxes, with the most lavish one at the top. A concrete ground floor contains wine storage and utility rooms; the second floor, which is clad in inexpensive paneling with an overlay of plastic insect screening, contains three bedrooms and bathrooms; and the top floor, which houses the living and dining rooms and kitchen, is a glass box with a small atrium at its center. "It's like living in a tree but being sheltered," Riehm says.

Although the living areas have motorized shades for use on warm, sunny days, privacy is provided by the trees, which look almost like scenic wallpaper. The atrium acts as a natural chimney to vent hot air out of the house (although there is air conditioning); its spiral staircase leads to a roof deck with panoramic views.

The guest house is a less costly version of the main house's glass box. With its open living-kitchen area and one bedroom, it looks like an International Style dollhouse. Piscuskas and Riehm have skillfully balanced modesty and luxury in their design, using the latter only where it counts — which, in a part of the world where excess has become commonplace, is refreshing.

Previous page: The glass-walled top floor of this Long Island house by 1100 Architect makes it seem as if you are dining among the treetops. Top left and bottom right: A dramatic staircase winds through the house. Its wooden treads are cantilevered from the wall, so that they appear to float in midair. Top right: The house is well hidden by the woods that surround it. Opposite page: The open-plan top floor contains the living and dining areas, as well as the kitchen. The epoxy floors are impervious to sand, spills, and children. The furnishings are a blend of vintage modernist and contemporary pieces.

Above: The pool house contains changing rooms and storage; its overhanging roof provides a canopy for eating meals prepared in the outdoor kitchen at left. **Left:** A view from the dining area, across the open-air atrium, to the kitchen. Sliding glass doors on both sides allow cross-ventilation. **Opposite page:** In the kitchen, a wall of walnut cabinets contains the refrigerator, freezer drawers, and food and appliance storage.

HOW TO HIDE A HOUSE: KALKIN HOUSE

NEW JERSEY

Photographs by Peter Aaron

It's not the sort of house you'd expect to find in a leafy New Jersey town: a big, galvanized-steel shed that would seem more at home in an industrial park. But that's only the beginning. Lift up one of the shed's big garage doors and you find a tiny clapboard cottage — much more in keeping with this part of the world — at one end of the cavernous space. But at the other end is a twenty-seven-foot-high, thirty-three-foot-wide grid of nine rooms that looks like a cross between a 1950s elementary school and the set of *Hollywood Squares*. In the space between the cottage and the grid, there is arranged the kind of elegant furniture that you find in a nice suburban house — where the owners could avail themselves of the services of a very good decorator. So what is this place?

It's the home — and brainchild — of Adam Kalkin, an architectural designer and artist who leads a peaceful life there with his wife, Adele, an elementary-school teacher, and their children. Their house was decorated by Albert Hadley, the dean of American interior designers — who, although known for his idiosyncratic chic, is not one for weirdness. It is this contrast between the Kalkins' comfortable existence and the unlikely structure that contains it that turns the act of everyday living into something like performance art.

But then, placing things in unexpected contexts is what Kalkin loves to do; he once staged a performance piece in a storage container that he hauled around Manhattan. And in this case, he knew the existing context well. Kalkin's parents' house is just down the road, and both their land and his were once part of a huge estate; the little cottage that now lives inside the big shed was built in the 1880s by the estate's gardener.

"You go to a new place, and you mark your territory, like an animal," Kalkin says. So, apart from adding the shed, Kalkin tore down most of a 1940s addition to the cottage, while leaving its foundation and fireplace, and inserted a house-shaped expanse of glass in the new metal structure where the addition used to be.

This combination of sign and ruin isn't exactly pretty, but that's not the point. "What a building looks like is not an interesting question to me," Kalkin explains. "It's like starting out at the end."

So when you ask Kalkin why his house looks the way it does, his answers have little to do with aesthetics. Why an industrial metal shed? "I've been interested in prefabricated structures," he says. Why put the cottage inside a shed, rather than just add to it? "I never thought about putting a building inside a building. I made a big space that would be a counterpoint to some smaller spaces." Why the grid of rooms? "It has to do with repetition. I originally toyed with the idea of stacking prefabricated prison cells. I wanted a different feeling from the rest of the house." Kalkin draws an analogy to cities, where there is a diversity of urban spaces. In Kalkin's domestic townscape, the stack of rooms is like an apartment building, and from the cottage you catch glimpses into its rear windows. The open living room is the town square between the structures. It is an indoor-outdoor space, particularly when the big garage doors are open. "You're not aware of the roof, because it's thirty-one feet high," Kalkin says.

He credits Albert Hadley with making the house "much richer and more accessible to people who might not otherwise understand it." But for Hadley, who has also worked for Kalkin's parents, the house posed a refreshing challenge. "It's sort of nutsville to build a hangar over that tiny house," he says, but the resulting luxury of space "is what we all dream of these days." Hadley felt that the scale of the living room demanded a more neutral color scheme, while the more intimate spaces of the cottage and grid allowed for much more color. And he loves the way the house sits on its wooded site, "like a living sculpture in the landscape."

That would please Kalkin, who says that he wants to bring architecture "into the bigger questions of life, not just this hyperrational conversation. Given the possibilities," he adds, "why are most things done within such a narrow bandwidth?"

Preceding page: The Kalkin house is a big metal-and-glass shed with a surprise inside — a small clapboard cottage. Left: Giant glass garage doors roll up to create an open-air living room inside the shed. The cottage itself contains the kitchen, library, and two bedrooms. Albert Hadley's decorating is elegant — yet relaxed — and so matter-of-fact that you would think that everyone has a cottage in his or her living room.

Above: A spacious, modern kitchen looks out from the cottage into the main space of the shed. **Below:** Albert Hadley's Fireworks wallpaper lines the master bedroom on the second floor of the cottage. **Opposite page:** Across the living room from the cottage, Adam Kalkin designed a concrete, aluminum, and glass grid of nine rooms. Kalkin sees the open space between the grid and the cottage as a sort of town square, particularly when the big garage doors are open.

FULL DISCLOSURE:
RADZINER-COTTLE HOUSE

VENICE, CALIFORNIA

Photographs by Dominique Vorillon

Southern California is full of concrete and glass houses: immaculate, slick, sparely furnished, and often cold as ice. At first glance, the architect Ron Radziner's own house in Venice, California — which he designed for himself; his wife, Robin Cottle, a graphic designer; and their two young children, Asher and Lexi — might seem like just another of these minimalist boxes. But look again. Sure, it's meticulously designed, with pared-down, dark-toned furniture carefully arranged in its open, high-ceilinged living-dining-kitchen space. But that space looks, through a wall of sliding glass doors, into a deep green, lushly planted garden. And what appears from a distance to look an awful lot like a carport projecting from the house's side is actually an outdoor dining room, complete with an enormous fireplace, topped by a master bedroom that hovers over the garden like some kind of elegant treehouse. In the evening, you can dine outside by the fire and look into the living area, a generous space glowing in the dark. Cool it is; cold it's not.

Radziner knows well what makes modernist houses livable; his firm, Marmol Radziner and Associates, has renovated or restored houses by twentieth-century masters such as Richard Neutra and R. M. Schindler, for clients like Tom Ford and Steven Meisel. Not that Radziner has the kind of budget these clients do: "For me to be able to execute this," he says, "it had to be quite spare." But California modernism promoted indoor-outdoor living, an idea that appealed to Radziner, and rather than focus on luxurious materials and details, he explains, "I wanted to put the money into the space and the garden." Landscape, he adds, creates exterior rooms, "which are as important as living rooms or bedrooms."

The twenty-four-hundred-square-foot house, modest by today's standards, is a wood-and-steel structure coated with a cement plaster tinted greenish gray. "I prefer a dark gray box sitting on the landscape to a white box," Radziner says. "I'd rather it recede a little bit." The architect's low-key attitude extends to the house's surroundings as well. To help the house harmonize with its predominantly one-story neighbors, Radziner made it one story tall in the front and two in the back (which contains Cottle's office downstairs and the bedrooms upstairs). And to maximize outdoor space on the 45-foot-wide, 130-foot-deep lot, Radziner placed the house along one edge and made it a mere 18 feet wide — the minimum width of a two-car garage, which local laws require in all new houses. This also allowed him to add the covered outdoor dining room that he felt would be a focal point. "The whole house opens onto it," he says.

Inside the main living space, concrete floors, white walls, and walnut cabinets — "They look barklike to me," Radziner says — form the backdrop for clean-lined furnishings, most of which Radziner designed and many of which

Preceding page: The design of Ron Radziner's house makes the most of a narrow lot by creating a spacious side yard. The projecting master bedroom on the second floor shelters an outdoor dining area below it. **Above:** A swimming pool is tucked into the back of the yard. **Right:** The house's airy, open main space contains a living area, dining area (in the foreground), and kitchen. Much of the furniture — including the child's table and stools — was designed by Radziner himself.

were made in Marmol Radziner's workshop. (The firm is also known for building its designs; half of the eighty people in the company are designers, and the rest are builders and craftspeople.) The open kitchen is equidistant from the indoor and outdoor dining areas, so that meals can migrate with the weather. The master bedroom is similarly spare, but the children's rooms are a bit more whimsical and colorful, although still decidedly modern: it isn't every child's room that has its own Saarinen or Bertoia furniture.

But if this house exudes youthful cool, it still seems like the kind of place a family can call home. Children wander freely between the garden and the living room, and on a warm, sunny day, the house seems more like an open-air pavilion. "Sometimes visitors look confused, as if they're wondering where the front door is," Radziner says. "For me,

it's the front gate. Once we buzz people in, they're in the house." It's not a concept that everyone grasps, however. "Even when the sliding glass doors are all open, people are still looking for that solid wood door," Radziner explains.

Radziner's firm has designed projects that range from schools to stores to private residences, including the ongoing restoration of Schindler's famous Kings Road house in West Hollywood. And while this variety of scale pleases him, Radziner loves working on houses and does not, as some architects do, see them as something to keep himself busy until bigger commissions come along. "There's something emotional and expressive about them," he says. "I never *not* want to do houses. I enjoy the intimacy of it."

Top left: In a child's room, stuffed animals congregate in a tepee, and classic modernist furniture blends with toys and games. Top right: The outdoor dining area offers a shady spot for lunch. At night, the open fireplace provides light and warmth. In its seamless connection of indoors and outdoors, this house is a descendant of the pioneering modernist houses that were built in southern California in the mid-twentieth century. Bottom right: In the white-tiled master bathroom, a transom tilts open to let steam out of the shower enclosure, and a large sliding window lets ocean breezes in. Opposite page: The open kitchen is convenient to both the indoor and outdoor dining areas. The Radziner-designed furniture echoes the cool, rectilinear forms of the architecture. The inside-outside connection is strong; Radziner considers the yard an outdoor living room. Thus, there is no conventional front door: you just open one of the sliding glass doors. (The front gate is always locked.)

GARDEN PAVILION: TARR HOUSE

EAST HAMPTON, NEW YORK

Photographs by Scott Frances

i
t isn't easy to design a house that's both monumental and intimate. A firm grasp of proportion is crucial; so is an informed deference toward the landscape. This eight-thousand-square-foot house on eleven acres in East Hampton, designed for Jeff and Patsy Tarr, exemplifies both. Its architect, Salvatore LaRosa of B Five Studio, and its landscape architect, Douglas Reed (who is now a partner in the firm Reed Hilderbrand Associates), have achieved a seamless interaction between house and garden, with the result that each of the house's five main, rather grand rooms feels as comfortable — and as connected to the outdoors — as a gazebo.

One key to this harmonious arrangement was placing the clapboard-and-brick house so that it looked at — rather than sat on — the site's most voluptuous contours, chief among which is a green knoll crowned by a big purple beech tree. "The idea of setting a rational building into a romantic landscape was at the heart of the design," Reed explains.

But this rational house is sensual too. Each room is a distinct pavilion, in which carefully framed views of the landscape are visible from strategically placed seating areas. "I'm always pushing you outdoors," says LaRosa, who is also responsible for the decorating that emphasizes the interior's dressed-down luxury. And although the design is clearly contemporary, it isn't aggressive modernism, LaRosa insists. You want to touch it. He used natural materials, like stone for floors and wood for ceilings, maximizing their tactile effect by treating them as simply as possible. But the real triumph of these sumptuously proportioned rooms is their human scale. "You are constantly aware of your body's relationship to the architecture and to the landscape," LaRosa says. Less skillfully handled, this house would have looked pretentious instead of elegant. But, as LaRosa cheerfully puts it, what is grace, after all, except never losing your sense of appropriateness?

Preceding page: The living room of the Long Island house designed by Salvatore LaRosa of B Five Studio. Above: In the dining room, the fireplace mantel is supported by a limestone column in the shape of a tree trunk, which was designed by Bob Vogel of B Five Studio. Opposite page: The dining room overlooks a shallow pool. The Gazelle chairs and bronze table were designed by Dan Johnson in 1958; the chairs are his best-known design.

Above: The house, which appears to be a series of pavilions, looks at, rather than sits on, its site's most voluptuous contours. The master bedroom and sitting room are at the far left, the living room at the far right, and the dining room, with its gridded window, is in between. Right: An arm of a chair designed by LaRosa in the living room illustrates his meticulous sense of detail. Opposite page: A painting by Robert Mangold is the focal point of the living room, with its two walls of sliding windows. LaRosa deliberately kept the room's palette neutral; color comes from the art and the outdoors.

Top left: A porch off the family dining area overlooks the house's "backyard," a sculpture court that is framed by hedges. Bottom left: Under the cedar-slat ceiling of the master bedroom, a low divider wall, framed in oak and upholstered in a cotton fabric, doubles as a headboard with built-in storage. Opposite page: The dining room and the living room are connected by a glass-enclosed bridge that spans a shallow pool.

A CLEAN SWEEP: MEYER HOUSE

SONOMA COUNTY, CALIFORNIA

Photographs by Jason Schmidt

In the wine country north of San Francisco, more so than anywhere else in the country, commissioning a showplace modernist country house has become almost a competitive sport. Architects like the elder statesman Ricardo Legorreta, the art-world favorites Jacques Herzog and Pierre de Meuron, and the up-and-coming Michael Maltzan have all been tapped, by forward-thinking clients with ample budgets, to create avant-garde villas among the grapevines.

Byron Meyer is one such homeowner. Meyer, whose business is commercial-property management and whose passion is collecting contemporary art, asked Stanley Saitowitz to design a house on a large property in Sonoma County. Saitowitz, a professor of architecture at the University of California at Berkeley who is known for his site-sensitive brand of modernism, produced a curving swath of three linked buildings that conform to the land's rugged contours. The sixty-five-hundred-square-foot, steel-framed and galvanized-aluminum-clad house — which includes a main structure for the living and dining areas, kitchen, and study and separate buildings for the master bedroom and guest wing — is "basically about the landscape," says Saitowitz. He calls the stylistic aesthetic "a continuation of California Case Study modernism, where the systems of construction are also the forms."

Within the austere but light-drenched house, Michael Booth, a partner in the interior-design firm Babey Moulton Jue & Booth, used an array of no-nonsense, classic modern furnishings and a palette of warm, neutral colors that would neither disappear in the bright sun nor upstage works of art such as the seventeen-foot-high Sol LeWitt wall painting in the living room. "It's a masculine house," Booth says, "but it's full of quirky objects that reflect Byron's personality."

From the house's pool deck, with its sweeping views and sculptural landscape of olive trees and boulders by the Napa Valley garden guru Roger Warner, Meyer says that his house has an otherworldly quality. "It's like a gigantic sculpture," he explains. "I feel really good being here."

Preceding page: The living room of Byron Meyer's house, with the dining room a few steps down in the distance (and kitchen at right), has radiant-heated concrete floors; the curved wall that frames the kitchen is Venetian plaster. The steel beams are painted a warm brownish-red that is taken from the bark of the madrone trees that grow in the area. **Top right:** A view of the other end of the living room, with its wall painting by Sol LeWitt. The spiral staircase leads up to a game room and on to a bridge that connects to the master bedroom. **Bottom right:** Meyer's photography collection is displayed on rails in the library. **Opposite page:** The library, which is just off the living room, is framed by a low doorway that contrasts with the living room's high ceiling.

Above: A long, screened dining veranda connects the main house with the guest wing. The most straightforward illustration of the house's architectural style, it highlights the steel-beam structure, galvanized aluminum panels, and concrete floors that are used in much of the house. The dining tables were inspired by the furniture designs of the minimalist sculptor Donald Judd. **Below:** The exterior of the enclosed bridge that connects to the master bedroom, which is in a separate structure. The house's architect, Stanley Saitowitz, designed the home to conform to the site's hilly contours. **Opposite page:** The kitchen is a series of three parallel counters — one for eating and two for cooking — that follow the sweep of the house's lines.

Top left: The bridge that leads to the master bedroom contains three furniture pieces made from designs by Donald Judd, including a high-sided wood daybed, a copper chair, and a wood settee. The wood pieces were fabricated by Jeff Jamieson. **Top right:** Wooden furniture, built (also by Jamieson) after designs by Gerrit Rietveld, sits under a massive olive tree on the pool terrace, which has a panoramic view of the landscape. **Bottom right:** The house's staggered roof lines illustrate Saitowitz's architectural approach — an update of the modernist Case Study House aesthetic. **Opposite page:** Photographs by Mike Kelley hang in the master bedroom, where linen fabrics and sisal carpeting reflect the house's neutral, warm color palette. The angular chair was designed by the Swiss architect Mario Botta.

TRAVELING LIGHT:
FIFTH AVENUE APARTMENT

NEW YORK

Photographs by Scott Frances

i n architecture, as in life, it's better to make the most of what you have than to try to be something you're not. Just ask Kimberly Ackert, the architect who turned a twenty-five-hundred-square-foot apartment on Fifth Avenue — with plain-Jane architecture but a great view of Central Park — into a shimmering hall of mirrors. Ackert and her associate, Felice Grodin, were asked to transform a jumble of small spaces (that had once been two apartments) in a mundane, 1960s glazed-brick building into a pared-down, light-filled home for a couple and their young son. (The apartment's spare but glamorous furnishings were the work of the design firm Healing Barsanti.) The result combines the openness of a downtown loft with the elegant sparkle of uptown's tonier precincts without trying to tart up the apartment's boxy structure.

Ackert's clients actually liked the building because its postwar modernity lent itself to the kind of contemporary design aesthetic they sought for their own living spaces. Never mind that the spaces in buildings of this vintage have fairly awkward proportions, being generally wider than they are tall; that was the architect's challenge.

The first thing Ackert did was to gut the apartment, reducing the number of bedrooms from four to three (including a small study–guest room) and placing them off to the north and east edges of the space. The main space became an open living-dining-kitchen arrangement, with exposed structural columns and luxurious views of the treetops and Central Park West. "I decided to treat the park side of the apartment as one giant window," Ackert explains. "In the previous layout, the views were obscured; the master bedroom overlooked the park, and the master bathroom was in the middle of the space."

But Ackert didn't stop there. She paneled the living area's north and west walls with mirrored glass, acid-etched to reflect light rather than images into the room. (The same glass is used in the master bedroom.) She then used conventional mirrored glass on the window wall's returns (that is, the sides that abut the windows themselves). These mirrors create endless reflections of the park and the room, dissolving the distinction between indoors and out. "They collapse the views together," Ackert says.

To make the space seem taller than its eight and one-half feet, Ackert dropped the ceiling along the two long sides of the living area, thus making the ceiling in the center of the room appear higher by comparison. She also matched

the pale color of the bleached and stained oak floor to that of the window-wall cabinets that conceal radiators and air-conditioners. This creates, Ackert explains, the impression of "running the floor surface up the wall" without visual breaks.

The right-angled austerity of the space is broken only by the graceful contours of the furnishings chosen by Healing Barsanti, and by a stainless-steel mesh screen, designed by Ackert, that rolls out at an angle to create a sheer, subtle separation between the living and dining areas. For Ackert, this interiors project was a departure from her previous work, which includes a number of sustainable, energy-efficient buildings. But the goal was not so different. "My specialty is trying to maximize natural resources in general," she notes — even if those resources happen to be daylight and a killer view.

Preceding page: At one end of the living room of this Fifth Avenue apartment, a pair of sofas designed by Andrée Putman creates a room within the room and offers a view of Central Park. **Right:** Ackert used mirrored glass along the window wall to maximize the light; these mirrors create endless reflections of the view outside.

Above: In order to make the master bedroom as bright as possible, Ackert used an acid-etched mirrored glass, which reflects light but not images.
Right: A detail of the living room's sliding stainless-steel screens, which run on a track set into the ceiling. **Opposite page:** The apartment's furnishings, which were chosen by the interior design firm Healing Barsanti, add gentle curves that complement the architecture's clean lines.

OPEN HOUSE: VACATION HOUSE

IDAHO

Photographs by Mark Darley

t he countryside around Coeur d'Alene, Idaho, would not seem to indicate that architecture — at least the kind with a capital A — is much of a priority. In fact, apart from a few new colonial-style farmhouses that look as if they were airlifted in from a Connecticut suburb, most of what you see simply falls under the category of "buildings." So it's all the more surprising, after you've traveled some long, winding roads and come to the edge of a lake, to see an arresting house of concrete block. You enter through a nineteen-foot-high vaultlike steel front door and make your way along bare concrete floors around a massive wooden stair (which leads up to the master bedroom), and suddenly the space explodes into a double-height living area, with an enormous steel window that flips up, like some larger-than-life garage door, the better to showcase the spectacular view beyond.

It's something from a postcard, but edgier.

That's just what the house's owners, a physician and his wife from Spokane, Washington, wanted in a weekend cabin for themselves and their children. And that's why they chose the architect Tom Kundig, of the Seattle firm Olson Sundberg Kundig Allen, to design their house. The firm is known for its striking modernist dwellings — and for being the preferred architects to a virtual who's who of the Northwest's contemporary art collectors. But Kundig's residential designs constitute an even more daring subset of the firm's output; his clients tend to be people who don't mind taking a bit of a risk and don't worry about what the neighbors will think.

In this case, the neighbors are pretty close to the house, as lakeside cabins tend to be, but the twenty-six-hundred-square-foot building looks mainly at the water rather than at the woods around it. Apart from the big windows in the living room and master bedroom, much of the glass in the house is concentrated in a ribbon just under the roof, which pitches gently upward at the front and back of the house, to let in additional light and offer views of the sky. "So much of this part of the world is about the sky," explains Kundig, who grew up in Spokane, a little more than an hour away.

It's a big sky, but it's a big landscape, too, and the house — while not that large itself — makes a few major moves in response. The front door is almost surreally tall in proportion to the building, but when you step back into the woods, you see how well it responds to the scale of the trees around the house. Then, of course, there is the pivoting window in the twenty-two-foot-high living room. The steel-and-glass window measures twenty feet by thirty feet, and raising it is like raising the curtain on some show-stopping stage set of water and mountains. Given that the owners wanted a house that was like a tent that they could use in all four seasons, you could also call this the ultimate tent flap. The window is controlled by an elaborate piece of manually operated mechanical equipment (designed in collaboration with Phil Turner, of Turner Exhibits, near Seattle) that Kundig refers to as the Gizmo. Such fanciful contraptions — beautiful, but certainly retro in the age of remote controls and "smart" houses — are a Kundig specialty.

"There's a natural beauty in the way things work," he says. "It's primal. To make something that makes you stop and think, even momentarily, about how something moves or changes direction connects us intimately to the natural forces in our world."

Apart from this and one or two other architectural extravagances — such as the front door and the four-foot-diameter steel pipe that houses the living room fireplace and serves as a key structural component — the concrete-block-walled house has a somewhat spartan aura, although this is mitigated by certain modern conveniences, such as a stainless-steel kitchen that would be the envy of any chef. The master bedroom is a plywood box that "floats" over half of the first floor, thus creating more-intimate spaces for the kitchen and television area, in contrast to the soaring space of the living room. But Kundig maintains that concrete and steel aren't as tough as they look. "These

Preceding page: This Idaho cabin has a giant glass-and-steel window that pivots open to provide unobstructed views of the lake. **Above:** The red sectional sofa adds a luxurious touch to the cabin's spare concrete-block, wood, and steel structure. The view from the living area at dusk seems almost larger than life. **Opposite page:** The twenty-by-thirty-foot window is manually operated by an elaborate piece of equipment that Tom Kundig, the house's architect, calls the Gizmo. Such contraptions are a hallmark of Kundig's houses, and their old-fashioned mechanical quality is all the more striking in our electronic age.

materials get better with age," he explains. "Oxidizing steel is like oxidizing tree bark. And the concrete block picks up the fungi and lichens that are on the site." (He's talking about the house's exterior, of course.) Moreover, he says, "concrete block has a human scale and makes a good connection between the big scale of the room and the nature of the house as a family place. These materials are totally no-maintenance."

Indeed, it's a house that scoffs at sandy feet and snow-covered boots and — for all its cutting-edge design — is warm and comfortable. "This is a very positive-energy kind of family," Kundig says. "They wanted a place that you would walk into and smile."

Above: The open kitchen, which is located along the wall farthest from the view, is made mostly of stainless steel and includes a restaurant dishwashing sink as well as a Craftsman utility chest that is used for storing cutlery and other essentials.
Opposite page: A length of steel pipe four feet in diameter contains the fireplace and acts as a structural component. The rough patch in the floor is actually the top of a rock similar to the ones found on the beach; the concrete floor was poured around it.

Top left: Another of the house's architectural extravagances is its nineteen-foot-high steel entrance door, which opens directly into a narrow hallway with a wood staircase that leads to the second-floor master bedroom. The house's roof seems to float on a ribbon of glass that lets light in and gives the rooms views of the sky.
Top right: In Kundig's hands, objects such as the box of light switches, which would normally be concealed in a wall, are pieces to be admired.
Bottom left: Part of the Gizmo is bolted to the concrete-block wall in the living room. **Opposite page:** In the children's bunk room, a plywood bookcase doubles as a ladder, and exposed electrical conduit becomes a playful sculpture.

PERSONALITY PROFILES

One of the most fascinating parts of my job is seeing how other people live. And a very special aspect of that particular "perk" is seeing how people with genuine personal style live. These people may be designers, but not always. They may live lavishly, or more modestly; money is far from the biggest factor in making a room speak eloquently of its owner. Indeed, I've seen many a house or apartment on which huge sums were spent, yet there was little warmth or personality — you might just as well have been in a very expensive hotel suite. The warmest, most interesting, and most stylish rooms are the product of a discerning eye and firm opinions. Great decorating is not for the namby-pamby.

The best decorators — amateurs as well as professionals — are almost always born with an instinct for beauty and have been trained in some way to express that instinct in line, color, texture, and proportion. It's no accident that of the seven houses and apartments in this section, three belong to architects or designers, two to collectors of art and decorative arts, one to an artist, and one to an actor who is also a noted photographer. For these people, the act of seeing is not something to be taken for granted; it's their gift and their art. They, by example, can teach the rest of us how to see.

These days, it's hard to find someone who isn't interested in design. New decorating magazines are sprouting up like daisies in a field, and television is chockablock with design programs: on home makeovers, do-it-yourself decorating, historic houses, vacation houses, and homes of the rich and famous, to name a few. Almost every major city in the country — and even some smaller ones — can claim at least one store devoted to contemporary design, and many more devoted to vintage furnishings. High-end specialty stores in the United States and Europe are taking a renewed interest in their home-furnishings departments. And even discount retailers — not previously famous for their interest in design — have joined in by hiring big design names, with the happy result that it is now possible to find a variety of well-designed products for the home at very reasonable prices and that design consumers are becoming better educated. At the same time, however, there seems to be a growing misconception that since design is everywhere, anyone can be a designer. All you have to do is express yourself.

If only it were that easy. That's not to say that no one should contemplate building or decorating a house without the services of an architect or designer; the reality is that relatively few people can afford them. But the way to learn the difference between good design and bad design — or between good design and great design — is to look at the best. The more you look, the better you'll learn to see. And you'll thank yourself for it one day, when you're sitting in a beautiful room, and it's yours.

A SAN FRANCISCO TREAT:
BOOTH-BEARD HOUSE

SAN FRANCISCO

Photographs by Mark Darley

t he best design is the kind that makes you look twice. How else would you see all the small, careful decisions that went into what looks like a single, authoritative one? Take this San Francisco house, which was designed by Michael Booth and Richard Beard for their own use. (They have since sold this house and designed another, also in San Francisco.) What strikes you first is its lanky, unassuming elegance. Its outside is the product of perfectly ordinary elements — weathered-cedar siding and double-hung windows. But the windows are overscaled, making the narrow, three-story front seem taller than it really is and setting the house apart from its densely packed neighbors on the hillside street.

Of course, the wood-framed windows are not just there to impress passersby. They are (on the top floor) the big exterior move that describes the big interior move — the house's thirteen-foot-high living room.

This room is so handsomely proportioned that you feel taller and thinner just standing in it. The furniture reflects Booth's deceptively casual, mix-it-up style, behind which lurks a keen attention to nuance. Thus, an austerely modern Mies van der Rohe chair, a sofa covered in sumptuous Fortuny fabric, and a simple Italian Chiavari chair seem made for one another.

The other rooms of the house (master bedroom, kitchen, and two smaller bedrooms, staggered in a split-level arrangement dictated by the sloping site) are modest by comparison. But faced with the usual gap between aspirations and means, Booth (a partner in the interior-design firm Babey Moulton Jue & Booth) and Beard (a partner in the firm BAR Architects) focused their resources on the nonnegotiables. These were the big living room, a kitchen that opened directly onto a garden ("my suburban fantasy," Booth jokes), and good-quality windows, which, although they ate up a considerable portion of the budget, were deemed too important to skimp on.

The house's subdued stylishness owes a clear debt to the work of such modern Bay Area masters as William Wurster and Joseph Esherick. Booth and Beard admire their architecture for its subtle sophistication. "It isn't flashy," Beard explains. "Nothing about it slaps you in the face, and it has integrity."

Just like this house.

Preceding page: On the facade of the house, elegant proportions add a certain grandeur to elements as ordinary as double-hung windows. **Top left:** In the living room, a false window is mirrored to balance the real window on the opposite wall. **Top right:** A corner of the living room doubles as a book-lined dining area. **Bottom left:** At the entrance to the living room, a Mies van der Rohe Barcelona daybed doubles as a stylish dog bed. **Opposite page:** The tall windows on the front of the house flood the thirteen-foot-high living room with daylight. But even at night, the pale yellow walls, warm woods, natural sisal carpeting, and neutral fabric colors give the room a honeyed glow.

Left: A tall doorway in the living room frames a view of the kitchen, which is down half a level, and the master bedroom, which is up half a level.
Above: An antique dresser and side chair stand side by side in the master bedroom.

Above and opposite page: The kitchen, which looks onto a small garden, is filled with art, favorite objects, and a comfortably stylish mixture of furniture, from the homey (the Italian Chiavari chair, with its gentle curves) to the high design (Gerrit Rietveld's Zigzag chair).

THEY DID IT THEIR WAY:
DE MENIL HOUSE

HOUSTON

Photographs by William Abranowicz

Two things stand out about John and Dominique de Menil's house in Houston. The first is that the 1949 Philip Johnson–designed dwelling still seems startlingly alive, long after Dominique's death in 1997. (Her husband died in 1973, and the house is currently maintained by the Menil Foundation.) A long, low antique Italian sofa still welcomes visitors in the spacious foyer. In the living room, a sinuous chaise longue by the great couturier Charles James, who decorated the house, beckons near the tall sliding window. Books on philosophy, religion, and poetry still pack the bookcases. And paintings by twentieth-century masters still hang on the walls. You half expect Dominique — with her delicate features and the ethereal bearing that veiled a keen mind and an iron will — to appear at any moment.

The second striking thing about the house is the contrast between its material splendor — suave modern architecture, jaw-dropping art, and serious furniture — and its casual down-to-earth aura. But this combination of elegance and unpretentiousness simply mirrors that of its owners.

John and Dominique de Menil — who in the early forties left France for Houston, where John (Anglicized from Jean) worked for Schlumberger Limited, the oil-drilling-equipment empire founded by Dominique's father and uncle — were two of this century's greatest art collectors. They cast their educated and refined eyes on quarry as diverse as surrealist paintings, African sculpture, and Byzantine icons — not to mention modern architecture. And they left a profound stamp on the cultural life of their adopted hometown.

But for all their sophistication (house guests included René Magritte and Roberto Rossellini), their philanthropic accomplishments (they were major patrons of two Houston universities and supported civil and human rights causes), and the stunning quality of their holdings (for which Dominique eventually built a remarkable museum, the Menil Collection), the de Menils shared a hatred of ostentation that bordered on the eccentric. She kept her clothes for decades and was known to wear her mink coat inside out; when he died, his plain wood coffin was carried in the back of a Volkswagen bus.

So when, in the late forties, it came time to build a house for themselves and their five children, John and Dominique predictably spurned the mock-Tudor and sham-chateau brand of design that prevailed in River Oaks, Houston's most fashionable neighborhood. "They believed in having the real thing, as opposed to the pseudo thing," recalls the de Menils' younger son, François, an architect.

John loved modern architecture; Philip Johnson, the "young" architect they chose for the job, was a disciple of Mies van der Rohe. Johnson designed a long, low, fifty-nine-hundred-square-foot, five-bedroom pink brick box with a flat roof, a windowless front facade, a back side with huge windows, and a small interior garden. While it was hardly the biggest new house in River Oaks, its impact was enormous. "A generation of young Houston architects in the 1950s" embraced the Miesian esthetic after Johnson introduced it, according to Stephen Fox, a Rice University architectural historian.

The de Menils loved Johnson's design, but — with the tough-mindedness that those who clashed with them called a mania for control — they tinkered with it anyway. Dominique, whom Johnson once called "the strongest woman in the United States," insisted (not unreasonably) on putting windows in the kitchen so that she or the servants would be able to look out, but this spoiled the symmetry of Johnson's facade. Most important, the couple couldn't live with the Miesian approach to interiors that reached its minimalist apotheosis in the Glass House, which Johnson was building for himself at the same time in New Canaan, Connecticut.

"The house was an example of their always aiming high, picking the up-and-coming brilliant architect," says the de Menils' oldest child, Christophe, who designs costumes for the composer-artist Robert Wilson. "But when we moved in, they felt it was a bit too exposed."

So John made the unlikely suggestion that Charles James — the maverick fashion designer whose mastery of cut drew comparisons to that of Balenciaga, and who had made many dresses for Dominique — be brought in to decorate the house.

Numerous accounts of the project had Johnson displeased with the choice of James, a fact that later seemed to baffle the architect. "I was delighted with what Charles James did," he insisted. "Isn't that funny?" In any event, architect and client remained cordial; the de Menils, whom Johnson said were "my biggest backers, my greatest friends," later commissioned him to design the Rothko

Preceding page: Dominique de Menil used to steam her Charles James gowns on the shower-curtain rod in her bathroom. James, who decorated the de Menil house, made the red velvet curtain in lieu of a bathroom door. **Right:** James's sensual effect on Johnson's modern architecture is apparent in the view from the foyer into the living room. The courtyard's dense foliage is echoed in the green upholstery of the Venetian rococo sofa at left. The large painting is by Yves Klein. Dominique frequently rotated the art on display so that no one would take it for granted. Black floor tiles are used throughout the house.

Above: The front facade of the house, which was designed by the architect Philip Johnson, is a long brick wall, broken only by the front door and the ribbonlike kitchen windows. **Opposite page:** James combined antiques — such as the seventeenth-century oak table, flanked by two Belter-style chairs — with his own designs, such as the seven-sided ottoman at the far end of the living room. The painting, titled *The Green Strip,* is by Mark Rothko.

Chapel (which he resigned from after a dispute with the artist). And the house helped pave the way for Johnson to become a major presence on Houston's skyline.

If Johnson did worry about what James would do to the house, he needn't have. James's legendary sense of form, color, and texture produced rooms that balanced the spareness of Johnson's architecture with a quirky sensuality. He designed curvaceous love seats (in addition to the chaise longue) for the living room. He used neutral colors in the main rooms and planted brighter-hued surprises — fuchsia, acid green, sky blue — in hallways, closets, and drawers. James urged Dominique to buy Belter-style furniture; its rococo revival complexity is all the more effective against the house's austere backdrop.

James was famously temperamental. The de Menils' second daughter, Adelaide, a photographer who collects tribal art, recalls that James would show up every day just as the painters, who had spent the morning awaiting his instructions, were taking their lunch break. James, furious, would then mix colors himself all afternoon until inspiration struck, by which time the light was almost gone. According to Christophe, "My sister and I had to hold flashlights so he could try the colors on the walls."

James had other, equally unorthodox working methods. Marguerite Barnes, a close friend of the de Menils' who was then an editor at the *Houston Post,* describes James's making a full-scale cardboard-and-brown-paper mock-up of the grand piano. "He said he couldn't start on the living room until he could 'feel the weight' of the piano," Barnes recalls. The family couldn't leave a packing box out for fear that it would vanish under James's paper Steinway.

Over time the de Menils filled the house with the paintings, sculpture, and objects for which they had developed a passion, thereby adding another layer to the idiosyncratic combination of modern architecture and eclectic decorat-

ing. Walter Hopps, the founding director of the Menil Collection, quipped, "Dominique was ahead of Philip Johnson on postmodernism," referring to the architect's notorious stylistic about-face in the eighties.

For two people who meticulously planned everything from art exhibitions (hers) to funerals (his), the de Menils were curiously silent on the subject of what should happen to their house after they died. With its extraordinary artistic pedigree, the house has become something of a cultural icon. And it was, as Hopps put it, the "DNA" from which the de Menil museum building, designed by the Italian architect Renzo Piano, emerged. Although the house sits on three prime acres of real estate, the Menil Foundation hasn't considered selling it off.

In fact, in 2004 (five years after these photographs were taken) the foundation completed an extensive renovation of the house, by the firm Stern and Bucek Architects, to restore the architecture and interiors, as much as possible, to their original state. The house is used only for special events and conferences; the family members who

Above: James's voluptuous love seat dominates the near end of the living room, where Picasso's *Buffet: Still Life with Glasses and Cherries* hangs above the fireplace. **Opposite page:** James designed a sinuous chaise covered in gray and acid yellow for the living room.

sit on the foundation's board didn't want their childhood home to become a house-museum. "The goal is not to have that kind of perfection," Adelaide says, "but to have the quirks and passions of real people." François agrees but strikes a more sanguine note. "Death by 'museification' would be a shame," he says. "You will never be able to re-create the aura of magic that people recall." His parents, he continues, "were not sentimental people — they were tough, and they went for the real."

Top right: Jean Dubuffet's *Texturologie III* hangs in the surprisingly modest master bedroom, just off the living room. **Bottom right:** James used bright colors for "hidden" places, such as in the hallway — lined in fuchsia velvet and pink and amber felt — that linked the living room and the children's rooms. **Opposite page:** A felt-covered door that separates the master bedroom from Dominique's dressing room has reminders and mementos attached to it.

FARM FRAÎCHE: GRANGE HOUSE

LOIRE VALLEY, FRANCE

Photographs by Jason Schmidt

a decorator's own house may not be his largest or most impressive project, but it is invariably one of his best, and certainly his quirkiest.

"It would have been impossible for me to do a house like this for anyone but myself," says the noted decorator Jacques Grange of the old barn he converted to a weekend retreat in the Loire Valley, less than an hour's ride by high-speed train from Paris. "It's too personal."

And that's saying a lot, since Grange's clients include people such as Yves Saint Laurent and Princess Caroline, who aren't exactly wallflowers. But as famous as Grange is for mixing antique and modern, high and low (like his renowned mentor, Madeleine Castaing), even the most daring client might shrink from the idiosyncratic juxtapositions of cultures and centuries that fill the three-story country home that Grange shares with Pierre Passebon, a dealer in twentieth-century furniture and decorative arts.

In the living room, which is at the same time cozy and airy (all of its windows look directly out to greenery — another Castaing inspiration), a rather grand-looking tufted sofa, covered in teal blue mohair velvet, is paired with a modernist cork-topped coffee table by the designer Paul Frankl and two rustic-looking chairs by Charlotte Perriand. Next to the sofa is an exquisitely minimal wood trestle table designed by Emilio Terry and a leather-covered lamp by Jean-Michel Frank. But the backdrop for this beyond-elegant arrangement is an almost funky wall of bookshelves made of plain pine boards to which Grange applied nineteenth-century mahogany pilasters.

In the master bedroom (which doubles as an informal screening room), stylish furniture and accessories by twentieth-century masters such as Jean Royère and Alexandre Noll meet François-Xavier Lalanne's famous sheep sculptures and a stuffed circus tiger — which, Grange hastens to add, died a natural death. In any other room, this design menagerie might seem overwhelming, but the room's enormous volume brings everything into balance. "*Le luxe* is the space," Grange explains, lapsing into his native tongue.

Grange's projects in the States include interiors for prominent clients, such as Ronald Lauder and Bruce Wasserstein, who prize the designer's knack for understated opulence. Now if only he could bottle his brand of fearless chic. That would be an import to reckon with.

Preceding page: A view from the living room of Jacques Grange's house into the kitchen. **Above:** The living room showcases Grange's gift for the mix. Rustic-looking wood-and-rush chairs by Charlotte Perriand sit opposite the luxurious blue mohair velvet sofa, and a modernist coffee table by Paul Frankl blends easily with a pair of Arts and Crafts–era lounge chairs. **Opposite page:** The refined lines of an Emilio Terry table and Jean-Michel Frank lamp offer a counterpoint to the layering of artworks, books, and objects behind them. The bookcases are made of inexpensive pine boards to which Grange applied nineteenth-century mahogany pilasters.

Right: One bedroom in the house is a shrine to the mostly American comic-strip art that is collected by Grange's partner, Pierre Passebon.
Below: Two bronze-and-wool sheep and a bronze donkey desk, all by François-Xavier Lalanne, inhabit the spacious master bedroom.
Opposite page: Also in the master bedroom, which doubles as a screening room, Grange mixed items as diverse as an armchair by Jean Royère, a photograph by Pierre et Gilles, and a stuffed tiger.

DRAWN FROM MEMORY:
GUSTAFSON HOUSE

LONG ISLAND

Photographs by Christoph Kicherer

i've spent many years telling people that in design, style is something that can be learned; you don't have to be born with it. But some people are — literally. Painted antique Swedish furniture is all the rage these days, and so is twentieth-century Scandinavian modern, but who would think to combine the two in one house? A Swede.

Mats Gustafson, an artist and a renowned fashion illustrator who has lived in this country for more than two decades, grew up in a house filled with such things (and with rugs that his mother designed). Since he understands almost instinctively the connection between a gracefully austere, painted Gustavian bench and a 1949 Hans Wegner dining chair, it's no big deal for him to mix them up in the cozy, unassuming Long Island house that he shares with his partner, the jewelry designer Ted Muehling. Here the antique and modern furniture you see spotlighted in pricey Manhattan store windows doesn't look special; it just looks right, and comfortable — not to mention somehow new when combined this way. In fact, the Swedes have a word for it: *lagom,* which Gustafson translates as "not too much, not too little."

Gustafson's austere, white-clapboard late-nineteenth-century farmhouse was a warren of small rooms when he bought it, so he asked two friends — the husband-and-wife architectural team of Solveig Fernlund and Neil Logan — for help. Fernlund and Logan redesigned the living areas to make them spacious and light-filled, but their interventions were so subtle that you'd swear the rooms had always looked that way — "like an Andrew Wyeth painting," according to Muehling. The architects also added a studio for Gustafson in the woods behind the house. For Gustafson, who for many years lived and worked in the same Manhattan loft space, the studio allows him to "devote all of the house to domesticity." Its spartan interior, illuminated by a skylight, seems a perfect, contemplative counterpoint to the house's homier clutter.

The rooms are filled with a mixture of pieces from Gustafson's family, his mother's rugs, ceramics designed by Muehling, and things that he and Muehling have found over the years. Muehling, who says he sometimes "likes a little Baroque," jokes that "a sheepskin thrown on a wooden bench is the history of Swedish luxury," but he also admires the elegance and restraint of Scandinavian design.

Of course, no room is built in a day; it evolves over time, along with its owners' personalities. Gustafson says that when he first came to New York, he rebelled against the coziness of his native design tradition, preferring a more minimalist, industrial look, "until I couldn't keep that side of me at bay any longer." But it's clear from these beautiful but unpretentious rooms that Gustafson must have known all along that there's no place like home.

Preceding page: The living room of Mats Gustafson's house. **Top left:** The kitchen, a room that manages to be homey and elegant at the same time. **Top right:** The guest room is furnished with Swedish Biedermeier pieces. **Bottom right:** The living room mantel holds a watercolor by Gustafson, ceramic objects by Ted Muehling, and the rocks and shells that have influenced the work of both men. **Opposite page:** The living room is a comfortable blend of antique and modern Scandinavian furniture; the Hans Wegner Y chair (better known as the Wishbone chair) is covered with a sheepskin — a typical Swedish touch. The rug was designed by Gustafson's mother, Inga-Kersti Gustafson.

Above: A view from the living room toward the kitchen shows how successfully Gustafson mixed old and new furnishings. The architects Solveig Fernlund and Neil Logan opened up the main living area, which had been a cluster of small rooms. Below: Fernlund and Logan also designed a studio for Gustafson behind the house. The modest clapboard structure fits neatly into the landscape of trees that have been the subject of many Gustafson watercolors. Opposite page: Watercolors of rocks are pinned to the wall of the studio, a serene, skylighted space.

HELTER SHELTER: LEIBOWITZ HOUSE

NEW YORK

Photographs by Jason Schmidt

t his Harlem town house is decorated to within an inch of its life, yet its rooms are obviously not the work of a professional decorator. Indeed, it's hard to think of a decorator with either the nerve or a sufficiently adventurous client to produce a place like this. These are spaces where op art–influenced wallpaper provides the backdrop for Warhol silk screens and flea market oil paintings. Where reproduction French furniture in the living room is covered in a fabric printed with black-power salutes. Where nineteenth-century photographic portraits mix with contemporary painting, and sofa cushions bear the image of Nelson Mandela. And where high-design objects such as chairs designed by Robert Venturi and Wendell Castle mingle with junk-store kitsch such as giant display bottles of liquor, presided over by portraits of George and Martha Washington. No, this is not the work of some pedigreed interior designer. This is Cary Leibowitz's world, and welcome to it.

Leibowitz, a print specialist at Christie's, bought his four-story (plus basement) 1894 house in the Hamilton Heights section of Harlem when his previous house in Brooklyn (purchased during the last real estate crash) became too small for his ever-growing accumulations of art, furniture, and artifacts of popular culture. Indeed, Leibowitz recalls that the actual move "ended up being an embarrassment in itself" because his possessions filled three moving vans. "As soon as it all got there, I thought, I hate this stuff, and have been giving a lot of it away," he says. But what is left — and there is an awful lot of it — tells an interesting story.

Growing up in suburban Trumbull, Connecticut, in the 1970s, Leibowitz did not, by his own account, "really have friends." He did, however, have a subscription to *Architectural Digest* — at age ten. He admired the work of such decorators as Mario Buatta, Thomas Britt, and Albert Hadley, and fantasized about the rooms designed by that goddess of twentieth-century style, Pauline de Rothschild. "I liked rooms that had traditional glamour and that were modern, but not too modern," he recalls.

When Leibowitz reached college age, he felt the need to justify his aesthetic choices intellectually. He gravitated to the work of the renowned postmodern architects and theorists Robert Venturi and Denise Scott Brown, because it looked "so smart and so subtle." Their interest in human scale and decoration was not shared by his architecture teachers at Pratt Institute, so he enrolled in the interior design program at the Fashion Institute of Technology, where the legendary professor Stanley Barrows didn't see eye to eye with him either. "I was idolizing Venturi's 'ugly and ordinary' aesthetic," Leibowitz says, "but I didn't understand it when Barrows found my work ugly and ordinary."

A brief, unpleasant internship with a decorating firm propelled Leibowitz out of the design world and into the painting program at the University of Kansas. It was there that he seriously studied art for the first time (he still makes art, in the form of text-based pieces that he describes as "late-twentieth-century gay Dada") and also began collecting it. His first purchases, made for a few hundred dollars each on the installment plan, were a Sherrie Levine watercolor "from her appropriation phase" and a Starn Twins photographic collage of a gargoyle. "There was this kind of banality, but at the same time, they were drawing with their photograph," Leibowitz says. Soon art had also opened his eyes

Preceding page: The living room of Cary Leibowitz's Harlem town house is lined with 1960s wallpaper. Wendell Castle's 1969 Molar chair and a chair from Ettore Sottsass's Westside Collection for Knoll, from 1983, are grouped around a rug by Frank Stella. **Above:** A painting by Jonathan Borofsky hangs above Leibowitz's bed, which is covered with a baseball-card quilt by Darren Brown. At the foot of the bed, a Lucite trunk is filled with a collection of brightly colored pants. **Opposite page:** An Andy Warhol portrait of Robert Mapplethorpe hangs at the foot of the staircase, which is literally lined with art.

to the kinds of objects that are normally relegated to the realm of kitsch, like the giant liquor bottles. And from there, he reports with almost comic understatement, "things kind of snowballed."

Leibowitz became a regular at flea markets and thrift shops, buying not necessarily for a specific room but because he had a feeling that an item would come in handy one day — like the art nouveau–inspired 1960s dining room wallpaper, which caught his eye in a Belgian wallpaper store "that had been in business for three generations and had lots of inventory." A carpet designed by Frank Stella was too big for his last house, but Leibowitz bought it anyway; in the living room of the new house, "it became the nucleus for everything to shoot off of."

There is a certain postmodern irony to Leibowitz's rooms. Although his sensibility is thoroughly contemporary in its fondness for appropriation and pop culture references, his pattern-on-pattern, "Where's Waldo?" aesthetic is basically a hipper version of the late-Victorian look the house would have had when it was first built. But instead of potted palms, fringed silk throws, and swagged curtains, you find a plywood chair, with Sheraton-style ornament silk-screened onto its plastic-laminate veneer, backed up against a wall that looks like something from *Rowan and Martin's Laugh-In.*

But that's this year. There's no telling what Leibowitz's roving sensibility will snare next. Although he may have slowed down, he doesn't see himself retiring from the accumulation business and says, in dead earnestness, "I sometimes read about people like that, and I'm afraid for them."

Right: In the living room, Warhol's portraits of Jimmy Carter and his mother, Lillian, hang on either side of a mass-market-reproduction French secretary, and reproduction French chairs and a settee are covered in fabric with a black-power-salute print. The chair in the corner is Robert Venturi's Chippendale chair, designed for Knoll in the 1980s.

Top left: Robert Venturi's Sheraton chair, designed for Knoll. Top right: In the dining room, a silk screen of a cow by Andy Warhol sits next to various giant-size Campbell's soup cans, a reference to one of Warhol's best-known subjects. Bottom right: Leibowitz's gift for the incongruous puts portraits of George and Martha Washington on the dining room's 1960s wallpaper, above a display of liquor bottles on a vintage dresser. Opposite page: The dining room wallpaper has an art deco look, echoing the look of Venturi's Deco chairs, another design in his Knoll collection.

GREY'S ANATOMY: **GREY APARTMENT**

NEW YORK

Photographs by William Abranowicz

j oel Grey may be a successful actor, but he's also no stranger to architecture or decorating. Grey has been working with heavyweight designers like Albert Hadley and John Saladino for more than three decades and has lived with every style from traditional pattern-on-pattern to minimalist chic. But for his current abode, a light-drenched downtown loft that overlooks the Hudson River, Grey chose a different style — his own.

Step off the elevator and you encounter a spare and spacious entry populated by a few simple pieces of furniture and art — a quiet, contained space that sets you up perfectly for the sunny sweep of the living area, with its thirty feet of windows. The furnishings are comfortable, with simple graphic shapes that stand up to the concrete floors and the white walls. Evidence of Grey's passions — his photography collection, his own photographs (some of which were published in his 2003 book, *Pictures I Had to Take*), his favorite editions and flowers — are carefully arranged throughout this room, his bedroom, and his office. It doesn't look so much carefully decorated as it does precisely inhabited. Of all the places he has lived, Grey explains, "my friends say this place looks most me. It looks undone."

Of course, even the most undone-looking rooms are the product of careful thought and planning, and for this Grey had expert help. Andrew Pollock, the architect on the project, says that the goal of the design was "to maintain the rawness of the original concrete space." The plan of the apartment minimizes the gridlike arrangement of the concrete structural columns — and, Grey says, "ended up giving me what I never would have given myself, like the extravagant space in the bathroom." Jack Ceglic, an artist and designer and longtime friend of the actor's — he painted Grey's portrait in 1967 for one of Bloomingdale's famous model rooms — served as a self-described "catalyst" for Grey's vision of the ideal home. Grey calls Ceglic "a mentor and a muse," roles the designer was happy to play. "He knew how to use us," Ceglic recalls, "and that's a great talent." He adds that his client found most of the apartment's contents anyway. "I'd come in and move things around and suggest things."

For Grey the entire process of buying, designing, and moving into his new home was one of distillation. First, moving downtown was its own adventure. (Grey's previous home was a penthouse in the venerable Hotel des Artistes off Central Park West, designed by another of his mentors and muses, Tom Pritchard.) Downtown, he says, "felt right to me in terms of its ease, and it has a very European feeling." Grey bought the space before the building was even under construction, after seeing the developer's model. "There was nothing there," he recalls. "The site was a parking lot." But he knew that this was the place for him: "Over the years, I've become obsessed with light. Three years ago, I stood in this space when it was an empty shell; there were no windows, just concrete slabs. I stared at the frozen river and blue sky, and I saw that that palette was where I'd been leading all these years — that neutrality, that peace."

Once he started on the rooms, he knew his instinct was right. "I tried painting two of the walls colors, but they had to come down," he explains. "I wanted the people, the objects, the life, to be the life" in the space. The objects are a mixture of old and new: "The stuff I like stays with me, like friends." The space needed a couple of pieces that were bigger — like the white canvas-covered Italian sofa and the Joe D'Urso–designed dining table — but other pieces are indeed old acquaintances, such as the pair of black butterfly chairs that sat on the terrace of Grey's previous apartment, the vintage wicker chair that came from a house he lived in in Los Angeles, and the Vuitton trunks that Grey lived out of when he was on tour.

Some pieces are souvenirs of his past design collaborations, such as the antique gilt-framed mirror, an Albert Hadley find, and the sleek daybed by John Saladino in the office. Certain things, like the concrete tub in the bathroom, were objects of desire, but more often than not, Grey's wish list for the space had more to do with setting than with things. For example, he had the floor of the bedroom (which is open to the living room) raised so that he could sit up in bed every morning and see the river — a view that also dictated the placement of the banquette just beyond the kitchen, where Grey has coffee and reads the papers each morning.

For Grey — who freely admits that the first thing he does when he checks into some hotel rooms is to remove the bedspread and replace it with a plain white sheet to "neutralize the space" — such carefully orchestrated moves create the set on which daily life is played. "It's about getting up in the morning," he says, "and wanting to see what you like." He comes by this perfectionism honestly, he argues. "You are either visual or you're not." And not only does Grey accept this; he relishes it. "It's not a hardship," he insists. "It's a joy."

Preceding page: In the breakfast area of Joel Grey's loft, his photograph of a Prague railroad station hangs above a banquette. Left: The living room, with its eclectic but clean-lined furnishings — such as the combination of the classic Alvar Aalto chair in the foreground with the recycled plastic table by Ineke Hans — provides a neutral foil for the views of the Hudson River and for treasured objects such as *Lake*, a cloth piece by Richard Tuttle, and the antique mirror against the far wall.

Above: The master bathroom is luxuriously spacious, and the concrete tub offers river views.
Right: Just off the living room, the master bedroom has no doors and is raised so that Grey can sit up in bed each morning and see the river. Thomas Stokes's painting *Yellow Emergence* hangs next to the bed, above a Louis Vuitton trunk and a walnut stool by Charles and Ray Eames. A glimpse of Grey's office can be seen beyond the bedroom.

Left: Grey's office, where an old cabinet from Texas looks right at home next to a standing lamp by Isamu Noguchi and a daybed by John Saladino (from one of Grey's previous apartments). **Below:** The actor's desk is a carefully composed still life in which mundane items such as pens and a photographer's loupe share space with family photographs and memorabilia. **Opposite page:** The highly personal office is lined with photographs and posters, such as the one from Poland for *Cabaret,* as well as caricatures of the actor by Al Hirschfeld.

ORGANIZING PRINCIPLES:
FORMICA-HIEMSTRA APARTMENT

NEW YORK

Photographs by Bob Hiemstra

When the designer Michael Formica was a boy, he would take everything out of his family's living room and rearrange it. His mother was not amused. But Formica was only honing his gimlet eye — which, after studying industrial design in the 1970s, he turned toward decorating. These days he gets to arrange some pretty swell stuff: among his recent commissions is a spacious house in which nearly everything is museum quality. But even in a more modest setting — specifically, the Manhattan apartment he shares with the photographer Bob Hiemstra — Formica proves that it's not only what you have that counts but also where you put it.

Formica and Hiemstra's approximately two-thousand-square-foot home (which was designed by Formica and James Orsi) was made by combining three small apartments on one side of a 1950s brick building. The resulting space is long and narrow, what Formica jokingly calls "the world's most expensive railroad flat." But what the rooms lack in grandeur, they more than make up for in elegant precision. The west walls of the living room, dining room, and bedroom are reserved for displays of the couple's diverse collections of objects and art. In the living room, a terra-cotta circus figure by Elie Nadelman shares shelf space with a ceramic obelisk by Jonathan Adler; in the dining room, an austere gray steel bookcase is filled with twentieth-century Weller Coppertone pottery, not generally known as a must-have for modernists. And in the bedroom, Venini glass bottles sit side by side with wooden forks and spoons (albeit by the French designer Alexandre Noll) and folk-art objects. New and old, fancy and funky, high-design and junk-store finds are all part of the mix. "I like that you can't tell what some things are," says Formica. "It's not trophy decorating." What the designer really finds interesting, he explains, is "the dialogue that objects have with one another." And orchestrating that dialogue, he says, is "a three-dimensional manifestation of a thought process."

Formica continues: "Some people paint, some people sculpt. I put things together. Not that I consider myself an artist; if anything, I consider myself an editor." The furniture, designed by a star-studded cast of characters past and present — from William Haines and John Dickinson to Jean Nouvel and Marcel Wanders — satisfies his desire for things that "are quintessential examples of what they are" and "do what they do elegantly." And although he wants the result to look effortless, Formica doesn't mind expending the effort. "I love doing this. It makes me feel good. It's like finishing the crossword puzzle."

Preceding page: In the dining area of Michael Formica and Bob Hiemstra's apartment, a series of paintings by Marco Tirelli presides over a collection of Weller Coppertone pottery and a vintage Tommi Parzinger lamp. **Top left:** The view from the living room to the dining area is filled with twentieth-century design icons, including a dining table by the French architect Jean Nouvel, Mario Bellini's classic 1976 Cab dining chairs, and a Knotted Chair by Marcel Wanders. **Top right:** Dutch botanical prints hang on a dark gray-green wall in the living room. **Bottom right:** Marcel Wanders's lacy Crochet Table looks right at home against the apartment's perforated metal radiator covers and aluminum blinds. **Opposite page:** The living room shelves display an array of mostly white objects, such as the snake lamp by Frank Gehry and the grid sculpture by Sol LeWitt.

Above and opposite page: The same modular metal shelves that are used in the living room run the length of one bedroom wall. Here, they contain objects ranging from Venini glass bottles designed by Tapio Wirkkala to wooden forks and spoons by the French sculptor Alexandre Noll. The carefully edited mix of twentieth-century furniture includes a modernist lounge chair, a highly collectible pair of plaster tables by John Dickinson, and a pair of Karl Springer lamps.

Acknowledgments

This book would not exist if it weren't for the architects and designers whose wonderful work first appeared in the pages of *The New York Times Magazine,* or the photographers who captured that work so brilliantly. To all of them go my thanks and admiration.

Since I joined the *Times* in 1997, I have had the privilege of working under three extraordinary editors in chief: Jack Rosenthal, Adam Moss, and Gerald Marzorati. I have also worked under three equally extraordinary style editors: Holly Brubach, Amy M. Spindler, and Stefano Tonchi. I am extremely grateful for their support and encouragement. Andy Port not only edited (and skillfully so) most of the articles that became this book, but she also wrote most of their witty headlines. Thanks also to John Hyland and all my colleagues at the magazine for their intelligence, their hard work, and their esprit de corps. Finally, I would like to thank two more people at the *Times* — Susan Chira and Alex Ward — without whom this book would still be a daydream.

From the beginning, Bulfinch Press was a terrific collaborator. Jill Cohen, publisher; Kristen Schilo, senior editor; Eveline Chao, assistant editor; and Alyn Evans, production manager, are a formidable team who have made this book more fun than work with their professionalism, their enthusiasm, and their unflappable calm.

Last, but of course not least, I want to thank my parents for encouraging my love of beauty and quality, and my siblings (and sibling-in-law) for sharing my passion for design.

Credits

All photographs in this book, with the exception of those by Peter Aaron on pages 116–121, originally appeared in *The New York Times Magazine*.

© Peter Aaron / Esto: "How to Hide a House," pp. 116–121.

William Abranowicz: "They Did It Their Way," pp. 168–177; "Grey's Anatomy," pp. 198–205.

© Mark Darley / Esto: "Open House," pp. 150–157; "A San Francisco Treat," pp. 160–167.

Carlos Emilio: "The Grand Tour," pp. 18–23.

Scott Frances: "Compound Interest," pp. 24–31; "The Enchanted Cottage," pp. 62–69; "Garden Pavilion," pp. 128–135; "Traveling Light," pp. 144–149.

© Scott Frances / Esto: "The Great Indoors," pp. 32–39.

Bob Hiemstra: "Organizing Principles," pp. 206–211.

Christoph Kicherer: "Drawn from Memory," pp. 184–189.

Nikolas Koenig: "Sky Box," pp. 110–115.

Marie-Pierre Morel: "Small Wonder," pp. 76–83.

Jason Schmidt: "Summer Camp," pp. 46–53; "Le Shack," pp. 56–61; "The Red and the Black," pp. 84–89; "Caesar's Other Palace," pp. 90–95; "Floats Like a Butterfly," pp. 96–99; "A Labor of Love," pp. 102–109; "A Clean Sweep," pp. 136–143; "Farm Fraîche," pp. 178–183; "Helter Shelter," pp. 190–197.

Dominique Vorillon: "Full Disclosure," pp. 122–127.

William Waldron: "The Perfectionist," pp. 40–45; "Block Islands," pp. 70–75.

Vicente Wolf: "Posh Spice," pp. 12–17.

Index